A THEORETICAL FRAMEWORK FOR MONETARY ANALYSIS

A THEORETICAL FRAMEWORK FOR MONETARY ANALYSIS

MILTON FRIEDMAN
University of Chicago

NBER OCCASIONAL PAPER 112

NATIONAL BUREAU OF ECONOMIC RESEARCH
New York 1971

Distributed by Columbia University Press

New York and London

This is a study by the National Bureau of Economic Research based on two papers: "A Theoretical Framework for Monetary Analysis," and "A Monetary Theory of Nominal Income," which appeared in the *Journal of Political Economy*, Volume 78, Number 2, and Volume 79, Number 2, respectively.

Library of Congress Catalog Card Number: 77–150319
ISBN–87014–233–X
Printed in the United States of America

NATIONAL BUREAU OF ECONOMIC RESEARCH

CONTENTS

Introduction

1. The Quantity Theory: Nominal versus Real Quantity of Money   1

2. Quantity Equations   3

3. Supply of Money in Nominal Units   10

4. The Demand for Money   11

5. The Keynesian Challenge to the Quantity Theory   15

6. A Simple Common Model   29

7. The Missing Equation: Three Approaches   31

8. The Missing Equation: The Third Approach Examined   34

9. Some Dynamic Implications of the Monetary Theory of Nominal Income   40

10. Comparison of the Three Approaches   43

11. Correspondence of the Monetary Theory of Nominal Income with Experience   46

12. The Adjustment Process   48

13. An Illustration   55

14. Conclusion   61

Introduction

Every empirical study rests on a theoretical framework, on a set of tentative hypotheses that the evidence is designed to test or to adumbrate. It may help the reader of the series of monographs on money that Anna J. Schwartz and I have been writing to set out explicitly the general theoretical framework that underlies them.[1]

That framework is the quantity theory of money—a theory that has taken many different forms and traces back to the very beginning of systematic thinking about economic matters. It has probably been "tested" with quantitative data more extensively than any other set of propositions in formal economics—unless it be the negatively sloping demand curve. Nonetheless, the quantity theory has been a continual bone of contention. Until the past three decades, it was generally supported by serious students of economics, those whom we would today term professional economists, and rejected by laymen. However, the success of the Keynesian revolution led to its rejection by perhaps most professional economists. Only recently has it experienced a revival so that it once again commands the adherence of many professional economists. Both its acceptance and its rejection have been grounded basically on judgments about empirical regularities.

1. The Quantity Theory: Nominal versus Real Quantity of Money

In all its versions, the quantity theory rests on a distinction between the *nominal* quantity of money and the *real* quantity of money. The nominal quantity of money is the quantity expressed in whatever units are used

NOTE: This paper is adapted from chapter 2 of a National Bureau of Economic Research monograph by Anna J. Schwartz and myself, "Monetary Trends in the U.S. and the U.K.," which is near completion. The first five sections of this article draw heavily on Friedman (1968). I am, as always, heavily indebted to Anna Schwartz. I have also benefited from discussion of some parts of this article in a number of classes in monetary theory at the University of Chicago and a number of meetings of the Workshop in Money and Banking of the University of Chicago. H. G. Johnson read the semifinal draft and made many useful suggestions for revision.

I am grateful to the staff reading committee of the National Bureau: Irving B. Kravis, Chairman, Gary S. Becker, and Richard T. Selden, and to the reading committee of the National Bureau's Board of Directors: Otto Eckstein, Walter E. Hoadley, and James J. O'Leary.

I am also grateful to H. Irving Forman, who drew the figures, and to Joan R. Tron for seeing the manuscript through the press.

[1] Several reviewers of our *A Monetary History of the United States, 1867–1960* (Friedman and Schwartz 1963*b*) criticized us for not making the theoretical framework employed in that book explicit. This paper is largely a response to that criticism. See Culbertson (1964) and Meltzer (1965).

to designate money—talents, shekels, pounds, francs, lire, drachmas, dollars, and so on. The real quantity of money is the quantity expressed in terms of the volume of goods and services that the money will purchase.

There is no unique way to express the real quantity of money. One way to express it is in terms of a specified standard basket of goods and services. That is what is implicitly done when the real quantity of money is calculated by dividing the nominal quantity of money by a price index. The standard basket is then the basket the components of which are used as weights in computing the price index—generally, the basket purchased by some representative group in a base year.

A different way to express the real quantity of money is in terms of the time durations of the flows of goods and services the money could purchase. For a household, for example, the quantity of money can be expressed in terms of the number of weeks of the household's average level of consumption that it could finance with its money balances, or, alternatively, in terms of the number of weeks of its average income to which its money balances are equal. For a business enterprise, the real quantity of money it holds can be expressed in terms of the number of weeks of its average purchases, or of its average sales, or of its average expenditures on final productive services (net value added) to which its money balances are equal. For the community as a whole, the real quantity of money can be expressed in terms of the number of weeks of aggregate transactions of the community, or aggregate net output of the community, to which it is equal.

The reciprocal of any of this latter class of measures of the real quantity of money is a velocity of circulation for the corresponding unit or group of units. In every case, the calculation of the real quantity of money or of velocity is made at the set of prices prevailing at the date to which the calculation refers. These prices are the bridge between the nominal and the real quantity of money.

The quantity theory of money takes for granted that what ultimately matters to holders of money is the real quantity rather than the nominal quantity they hold and that there is a fairly definite real quantity of money that people wish to hold under any given circumstances. Suppose that the nominal quantity that people hold at a particular moment of time happens to correspond at current prices to a real quantity larger than the quantity that they wish to hold. Individuals will then seek to dispose of what they regard as their excess money balances; they will try to pay out a larger sum for the purchase of securities, goods and services, for the repayment of debts, and as gifts than they are receiving from the corresponding sources. However, they cannot as a group succeed. One man's expenditures are another's receipts. One man can reduce his nominal money balances only by persuading someone else to increase his. The community as a whole cannot in general spend more than it receives.

The attempt to do so will nonetheless have important effects. If prices and income are free to change, the attempt to spend more will raise the volume of expenditures and receipts, expressed in nominal units, which will lead to a bidding up of prices and perhaps also to an increase in output. If prices are fixed by custom or by government edict, the attempt to spend more will either be matched by an increase in goods and services or produce "shortages" and "queues." These, in turn, will raise the effective price and are likely sooner or later to force changes in official prices.

The initial excess of nominal balances will therefore tend to be eliminated, even though there is no change in the nominal quantity of money, by either a reduction in the real quantity available to hold through price rises or an increase in the real quantity desired through output increases. And conversely for an initial deficiency of nominal balances.

It is clear from this discussion that changes in prices and nominal income can be produced either by changes in the real balances that people wish to hold or by changes in the nominal balances available for them to hold. Indeed, it is a tautology, summarized in the famous quantity equation, that all changes in nominal income can be attributed to one or the other—just as a change in the price of any good can always be attributed to a change in either demand or supply. The quantity theory is not, however, this tautology. On an analytical level, it is an analysis of the factors determining the quantity of money the community wishes to hold; on an empirical level, it is the generalization that changes in desired real balances (in the demand for money) tend to proceed slowly and gradually or to be the result of events set in train by prior changes in supply, whereas, in contrast, substantial changes in the supply of nominal balances can and frequently do occur independently of any changes in demand. The conclusion is that substantial changes in prices or nominal income are almost invariably the result of changes in the nominal supply of money.

2. Quantity Equations

The tautology embodied in the quantity equation is a useful device for clarifying the variables stressed in the quantity theory. The quantity equation has taken different forms, according as quantity theorists have stressed different variables.

a) Transactions Equation

The most famous version of the quantity equation is doubtless the transactions version popularized by Irving Fisher (Fisher 1911, pp. 24–54):

$$MV = PT, \tag{1}$$

or

$$MV + M'V' = PT. \tag{2}$$

In this version, the elementary event is a transaction: an exchange in which one economic actor transfers to another economic actor goods or services or securities and receives a transfer of money in return. The right-hand side of the equations corresponds to the transfer of goods, services, and securities; the left-hand side, to the matching transfer of money.

Each transfer of goods, services, or securities is regarded as the product of a price and a quantity: wage per week times number of weeks, price of a good times number of units of the good, dividend per share times number of shares, price per share times number of shares, and so on. The right-hand side of equations (1) and (2) is the aggregate of such payments during some interval, with P a suitably chosen *average* of the prices, and T a suitably chosen *aggregate* of the quantities during that interval, so that PT is the total nominal value of the payments during the interval in question. The units of P are dollars per unit of quantity; the units of T are number of unit quantities per period of time. We can convert the equation from an expression applying to an *interval* of time to one applying as of a *point* in time by the usual limiting process of letting the interval of time for which we aggregate payments approach zero, and expressing T not as an aggregate but as a rate of flow (that is, the limit of the ratio of aggregate quantities to the length of the interval as the length of the interval approaches zero). The magnitude T then has the dimension of quantity per unit time. The product of P and T then has the dimension of dollars per unit time.

Because the right-hand side is intended to summarize a continuing process, a flow of physical goods and services, the physical item transferred (good, service, or security) is treated as if it disappeared from economic circulation once transferred. If, for example, a single item, say, a house, were transferred three times in the course of the time interval for which PT is measured, it would enter into T as three houses for that time interval. Further, only those physical items that enter into transactions are explicitly included in T. The houses that exist but are not bought or sold during the time interval are omitted, though, if they are rented, the rental values of their services will be included in PT and the number of dwelling-unit years per year will be included in T. Clearly, T is a rather special kind of index of quantities: it includes service flows (man-hours, dwelling-unit years, kilowatt hours) but also capital items yielding flows (houses, electric generating plants), weighting each of these capital items in accordance with the number of times it enters into exchanges (its "velocity of circulation" in strict analogy with the "velocity of circulation" of money). Similarly, P is a rather special kind of price index.

The monetary transfer analyzed on the left-hand side of equations (1) and (2) is treated very differently. The money that changes hands is treated as retaining its identity, and all money, whether used in transactions during the time interval in question or not, is explicitly accounted for. Money is treated as a stock, not a flow or a mixture of a flow and a stock. For a single transaction, the breakdown into M and V is trivial: the cash that is transferred is turned over once, or $V = 1$. For all transactions during an interval, we can, in principle, classify the existing stock of dollars of money according as each dollar entered into 0, 1, 2, . . . transactions, that is, according as each dollar "turned over" 0, 1, 2, . . . times. The weighted average of these numbers of turnover, weighted by the number of dollars that turned over that number of times, is the conceptual equivalent of V. The dimensions of M are dollars; of V, number of turnovers per unit time; so, of the product, dollars per unit time.[2]

Equation (2) differs from equation (1) by dividing payments into two categories: those effected by the transfer of hand-to-hand currency (including coin) and those effected by the transfer of deposits. In equation (2) M stands solely for the volume of currency and V for

[2] A common criticism of the quantity equation is that, while it takes account of the velocity of circulation of money, it does not take account of the velocity of circulation of goods. As the preceding two paragraphs make clear, while this criticism is not literally valid, it has a real point. The velocity of circulation of money is explicit; the velocity of circulation of goods is implicit. It might well make the right-hand side of equations (1) and (2) more meaningful to make it the sum of two components—one, the total value of transactions involving continuing flows, the other, the value of transfers of existing items of wealth—and to express the second component as a price times a velocity times a stock. In effect, the shift to the income version of the equation resolves the issue by completely neglecting transfers of existing items of wealth.

the velocity of currency, M' for the volume of deposits and V' for the velocity of deposits.

One reason for the emphasis on this particular division was the persistent dispute about whether the term "money" should include only currency or deposits as well (Friedman and Schwartz 1970, chap. 2). Another reason was the direct availability of figures on $M'V'$ from bank records of clearings or of debits to deposit accounts. These make it possible to calculate V' in a way that it is not possible to calculate V.[3]

Equations (1) and (2), like the other quantity equations I shall discuss, are intended to be identities—a special application of double-entry bookkeeping, with each transaction simultaneously recorded on both sides of the equation. However, as with the national income identities with which we are all familiar, when the two sides, or the separate elements on the two sides, are estimated from independent sources of data, many differences between the two sides emerge (Mitchell 1927, pp. 128–39). This has been less obvious for the quantity equations than for the national income identities—with their standard entry "statistical discrepancy"—because of the difficulty of calculating V directly. As a result, V in equation (1) or V and V' in equation (2) have generally been calculated as the numbers having the property that they render the equations correct. These calculated numbers therefore embody the whole of the counterpart to the "statistical discrepancy."

Just as the left-hand side of equation (1) can be divided into several components, as in equation (2), so also can the right-hand side. The emphasis on transactions reflected in this version of the quantity equation suggests dividing total transactions into categories of payments for which payment periods or practices differ: for example, into capital transactions, purchases of final goods and services, purchases of intermediate goods, payments for the use of resources, perhaps separated into wage and salary payments and other payments. The observed value of V might well be a function of the distribution of total payments among categories. Alternatively, if the quantity equation is interpreted not as an identity but as a functional relation expressing desired velocity as a function of other variables, the distribution of payments may well be an important set of variables.

b) The Income Form of the Quantity Equation

Despite the large amount of empirical work done on the transactions equations, notably by Irving Fisher and Carl Snyder (Fisher 1911, pp.

[3] For an extremely ingenious indirect calculation of V, not only for currency as a whole but for particular denominations of currency, see Laurent (1969).

280–318; Fisher 1919; Snyder 1934), the ambiguities of the concepts of "transactions" and the "general price level"—particularly those arising from the mixture of current and capital transactions—were never satisfactorily resolved. The more recent development of national or social accounting has stressed income transactions rather than gross transactions and has explicitly and satisfactorily dealt with the conceptual and statistical problems of distinguishing between changes in prices and changes in quantities. As a result, the quantity equation has more recently tended to be expressed in terms of income rather than of transactions. Let $Y =$ nominal national income, $P =$ the price index implicit in estimating national income at constant prices, and $y =$ national income in constant prices, so that

$$Y = Py. \tag{3}$$

Let M represent, as before, the stock of money; but define V as the average number of times per unit time that the money stock is used in making *income* transactions (that is, payments for final productive services or, alternatively, for final goods and services) rather than all transactions. We can then write the quantity equation in income form as

$$MV = Py, \tag{4}$$

or, if it is desired to distinguish currency from deposit transactions, as

$$MV + M'V' = Py. \tag{5}$$

Although the symbols P, V, and V' are used both in equations (4) and (5) and in equations (1) and (2), they stand for different concepts in each pair of equations.

Equations (4) and (5) are both conceptually and empirically more satisfactory than equations (1) and (2). However, they have the disadvantage that they completely neglect both the ratio of intermediate to final transactions and transactions in existing capital assets.

In the transactions version of the quantity equation, each intermediate transaction—that is, purchase by one enterprise from another—is included at the total value of the transaction, so that the value of wheat, for example, is included once when it is sold by the farmer to the mill, a second time when the mill sells flour to the baker, a third time when the baker sells bread to the grocer, a fourth time when the grocer sells bread to the consumer. In the income version, only the net value added by each of these transactions is included. To put it differently, in the transactions version, the elementary event is an isolated exchange of a physical item for money—an actual, clearly observable event. In the income version, the elementary event is a hypothetical event that can be inferred from observation but is not directly observable. It is a complete series of transactions involving the exchange of productive services for final goods, via a sequence of money payments, with all the intermediate transactions in this income circuit netted out. The total value of all transactions is therefore a multiple of the value of income transactions only.

For a given flow of productive services or, alternatively, of final products (two of the multiple faces of income), the volume of transactions will clearly be affected by vertical integration or disintegration of enterprises, which reduces or increases the number of transactions involved in a single income circuit, or by technological changes that lengthen or shorten the process of transforming productive services into final products. The volume of income will not be thus affected.

Similarly, the transactions version includes the purchase of an existing asset—a house or a piece of land or a share of equity stock—precisely on a par with an intermediate or final transaction. The income version excludes such transactions completely.

Are these differences an advantage or disadvantage of the income version? That clearly depends on what it is that determines the amount of money people want to hold. Do changes of the kind considered in the preceding paragraphs, changes that alter the ratio of intermediate and capital transactions to income, also alter in the same direction and by the same proportion the amount of money people want to hold? Or do they tend to leave this amount unaltered? Or do they have a more complex effect?

Clearly, the transactions and income versions of the quantity theory involve very different conceptions of the role of money. For the transactions version, the most important thing about money is that it is transferred. For the income version, the most important thing is that it is held. This difference is even more obvious from the Cambridge cash-balances version of the quantity equation. Indeed, the income version can perhaps best be regarded as a way station between the Fisher and the Cambridge versions.

c) Cambridge Cash-Balances Approach

The essential feature of a money economy is that it enables the act of purchase to be separated from the act of sale. An individual who has something to exchange need not seek out the double coincidence—someone who both wants what he has and offers in exchange what he wants. He need only find someone who wants what he has, sell it to him for general purchasing power, and then find someone who has what he wants and buy it with general purchasing power.

In order for the act of purchase to be separated from the act of sale, there must be something which everybody will accept in exchange as "general purchasing power"—this is the aspect of money emphasized in the transactions approach. But also there must be something which can serve as a temporary abode of purchasing power in the interim between sale and purchase. This is the aspect of money emphasized in the cash-balances approach.

How much money will people or enterprises want to hold for this purpose? As a first approximation, it has generally been supposed that the amount bears some relation to income, on the assumption that this affects the volume of potential purchases for which the individual or enterprise wishes to hold a temporary abode of purchasing power. We can therefore write

$$M = kPy, \tag{6}$$

where M, P, and y are defined as in equation (4), and k is the ratio of money stock to income—either the observed ratio so calculated as to make equation (6) an identity, or the "desired" ratio so that M is the "desired" amount of money, which need not be equal to the actual amount. In either case, k is numerically equal to the reciprocal of the V in equation (4), the V in one case being interpreted as measured velocity and in the other as desired velocity.

Although equation (6) is simply a mathematical transformation of equation (4), it brings out much more sharply the difference between the aspects of money stressed by the transactions approach and those stressed by the cash-balances approach. This difference makes different definitions of money seem natural and leads to emphasis being placed on different variables and analytical techniques.

The transactions approach makes it natural to define money in terms of whatever serves as the medium of exchange in discharging obligations. By stressing the function of money as a temporary abode of purchasing power, the cash-balances approach makes it seem entirely appropriate to include also such stores of value as demand and time deposits not transferable by check, although this approach clearly does not require their inclusion (Friedman and Schwartz 1970, chap. 3).

Similarly, the transactions approach leads to stress being placed on such variables as payments practices, the financial and economic arrangements for effecting transactions, and the speed of communication and transportation as it affects the time required to make a payment—essentially, that is, to emphasis on the mechanical aspects of the payments process. The cash-balances approach, on the other hand, leads to stress being placed on variables affecting the usefulness of money as an asset: the costs and returns from holding money instead of other assets, the uncertainty of the future, and so on—essentially, that is, to emphasis on the role of cash in a portfolio.

Of course, neither approach enforces the exclusion of the variables stressed by the other—and the more sophisticated economists who have used them have had broader conceptions than the particular approach they adopted. The portfolio aspects enter into the costs of effecting transactions and hence affect the most efficient payment arrangements; the mechanical aspects enter into the returns from holding cash and hence affect the usefulness of cash in a portfolio.

Finally, with regard to analytical techniques, the cash-balances approach fits in much more readily with the general Marshallian demand-supply apparatus than does the transactions approach. Equation (6) can be regarded as a demand function for money, with P and y on the right-hand side being two of the variables on which demand for money depends, and with k symbolizing all the other variables, so that k is to be regarded not as a numerical constant but as itself a function of still other variables. For completion, the analysis requires another equation showing the supply of money as a function of other variables. The price level or the level of nominal income is then the resultant of the interaction of the demand and supply functions.

The quantity theory in its cash-balances version thus suggests organizing an analysis of monetary phenomena in terms of (1) the factors determining the nominal quantity of money to be held—the conditions determining supply—and (2) the factors determining the real quantity of money the community wishes to hold—the conditions determining demand.

3. Supply of Money in Nominal Units

The factors determining the nominal quantity of money available to be held depend critically on the monetary system. For systems like those which have prevailed in the United States and in the United Kingdom during the past century, they can usefully be analyzed under the three main headings that we have termed the proximate determinants of the money stock: (1) the amount of high-powered money—for any one country this is determined through the balance of payments under an international commodity standard, by the monetary authorities, under a fiduciary standard; (2) the ratio of bank deposits to bank holdings of high-powered money—this is determined by the banking system subject to whatever requirements are imposed on them by law or the monetary authorities; and (3) the ratio of the public's deposits to its currency holdings—this is determined by the public (Friedman and Schwartz 1963*b*, pp. 776–98; Cagan 1965).

4. The Demand for Money

J. M. Keynes's liquidity preference analysis (discussed further in section 5, below) reinforced the shift of emphasis from the transactions version of the quantity equation to the cash-balances version—a shift of emphasis from mechanical aspects of the payments process to the qualities of money as an asset. Keynes's analysis, though strictly in the Cambridge cash-balances tradition, was much more explicit in stressing the role of money as one among many assets, and of interest rates as the relevant cost of holding money.

More recent work has gone still further in this direction, treating the demand for money as part of capital or wealth theory, concerned with the composition of the balance sheet or portfolio of assets.

From this point of view, it is important to distinguish between ultimate wealth holders, to whom money is one form in which they choose to hold their wealth, and enterprises, to whom money is a producer's good like machinery or inventories (Friedman 1956).

a) Demand by Ultimate Wealth Holders

For ultimate wealth holders, the demand for money, in real terms, may be expected to be a function primarily of the following variables:

i) *Total wealth.*—This is the analogue of the budget constraint in the usual theory of consumer choice. It is the total that must be divided among various forms of assets. In practice, estimates of total wealth are seldom available. Instead, income may serve as an index of wealth. However, it should be recognized that income as measured by statisticians may be a defective index of wealth because it is subject to erratic year-to-year fluctuations, and a longer-term concept, like the concept of permanent income developed in connection with the theory of consumption, may be more useful (Friedman 1957, 1959; Brunner and Meltzer 1963; Meltzer 1963).

The emphasis on income as a surrogate for wealth, rather than as a measure of the "work" to be done by money, is conceptually perhaps the basic difference between more recent work and the earlier versions of the quantity theory.

ii) *The division of wealth between human and nonhuman forms.*—The major asset of most wealth holders is their personal earning capacity, but the conversion of human into nonhuman wealth or the reverse is subject to narrow limits because of institutional constraints. It can be done by using current earnings to purchase nonhuman wealth or by using nonhuman wealth to finance the acquisition of skills but not by purchase or sale and to only a limited extent by borrowing on the collateral of earning power. Hence, the fraction of total wealth that is in the form of nonhuman wealth may be an additional important variable.

iii) *The expected rates of return on money and other assets.*—This is the analogue of the prices of a commodity and its substitutes and complements in the usual theory of consumer demand. The nominal rate of return on money may be zero, as it generally is on currency, or negative, as it sometimes is on demand deposits subject to net service charges, or positive, as it sometimes is on demand deposits on which interest is paid and generally is on time deposits. The nominal rate of return on other assets consists of two parts: first, any currently paid yield or cost, such as interest on bonds, dividends on equities, and storage costs on physical assets, and, second, changes in their nominal prices. The second part will, of course, be especially important under conditions of inflation or deflation.

iv) *Other variables determining the utility attached to the services rendered by money relative to those rendered by other assets—in Keynesian terminology, determining the value attached to liquidity proper.*—One such variable may be one already considered—namely, real wealth or income, since the services rendered by money may, in principle, be regarded by wealth holders as a "necessity," like bread, the consumption of which increases less than in proportion to any increase in income, or as a "luxury," like recreation, the consumption of which increases more than in proportion.

Another variable that is likely to be important empirically is the degree of economic stability expected to prevail in the future. Wealth holders are likely to attach considerably more value to liquidity when they expect economic conditions to be unstable than when they expect them to be highly stable. This variable is likely to be difficult to express quantitatively even though the direction of change may be clear from qualitative information. For example, the outbreak of war clearly produces expectations of instability, which is one reason why war is often accompanied by a notable increase in real balances—that is, a notable decline in velocity.

Still another variable may be the volume of capital transfers relative to income—of trading in existing capital goods by ultimate wealth holders. The higher the turnover of capital assets, the higher the fraction of total assets people may find it useful to hold as cash. This variable corresponds to the class of transactions neglected in going from the transactions version of the quantity equation to the income version.

We can symbolize this analysis in terms of the following demand function for money for an individual wealth holder:

$$\frac{M}{P} = f\left(y,\ w;\ r_m,\ r_b,\ r_e,\ \frac{1}{P}\frac{dP}{dt};\ u\right), \tag{7}$$

where M, P, and y have the same meaning as in equation (6) except that they relate to a single wealth holder; w is the fraction of wealth in nonhuman form (or, alternatively, the fraction of income derived from property); r_m is the expected nominal rate of return on money; r_b is the expected nominal rate of return on fixed-value securities, including expected changes in their prices; r_e is the expected nominal rate of return on equities, including expected changes in their prices; $(1/P)(dP/dt)$ is the expected rate of change of prices of goods and hence the expected nominal rate of return on real assets; and u is a portmanteau symbol standing for whatever variables other than income may affect the utility attached to the services of money. Each of the four rates of return stands, of course, for a set of rates of return, and for some purposes it may be important to classify assets still more finely —for example, to distinguish currency from deposits, long-term from short-term fixed-value securities, risky from relatively safe equities, and one kind of physical assets from another.[4]

The usual problems of aggregation arise in passing from equation (7) to a corresponding equation for the economy as a whole—in particular, they arise from the possibility that the amount of money demanded may depend on the distribution among individuals of such variables as y and w and not merely on their aggregate or average value. If we neglect these distributional effects, equation (7) can be

---

[4] Under some assumed conditions, the four rates of return may not be independent. For example, in a special case considered in Friedman (1956, pp. 9–10),

$$r_b = r_e + (1/P)(dP/dt).$$

regarded as applying to the community as a whole, with M and y referring to per capita money holdings and per capita real income, respectively, and w to the fraction of aggregate wealth in nonhuman form.

The major problems that arise in practice in applying equation (7) are the precise definitions of y and w, the estimation of *expected* rates of return as contrasted with actual rates of return, and the quantitative specification of the variables designated by u.

b) *Demand by Business Enterprises*

Business enterprises are not subject to a constraint comparable with that imposed by the total wealth of the ultimate wealth holder. The total amount of capital embodied in productive assets, including money, is a variable that can be determined by an enterprise to maximize returns, since it can acquire additional capital through the capital market. Hence, there is no reason on this ground to include total wealth, or y as a surrogate for total wealth, as a variable in the business demand function for money.

It may, however, be desirable to include a somewhat similar variable defining the "scale" of the enterprise on different grounds—namely, as an index of the productive value of different quantities of money to the enterprise. This is more nearly in line with the earlier transactions approach emphasizing the "work" to be done by money. It is by no means clear what the appropriate variable is: total transactions, net value added, net income, total capital in nonmoney form, or net worth. The lack of availability of data has meant that much less empirical work has been done on the business demand for money than on an aggregate demand curve encompassing both ultimate wealth holders and business enterprises. As a result there are as yet only faint indications about the best variable to use.

The division of wealth between human and nonhuman form has no special relevance to business enterprises, since they are likely to buy the services of both forms on the market.

Rates of return on money and on alternative assets are, of course, highly relevant to business enterprises. These rates determine the net cost to them of holding the money balances. However, the particular rates that are relevant may be quite different from those that are relevant for ultimate wealth holders. For example, rates charged by banks on loans are of minor importance for wealth holders yet may be extremely important for businesses, since bank loans may be a way in which they can acquire the capital embodied in money balances.

The counterpart for business enterprises of the variable u in equation

(7) is the set of variables other than scale affecting the productivity of money balances. At least one of these—namely, expectations about economic stability—is likely to be common to business enterprises and ultimate wealth holders.

With these interpretations of the variables, equation (7), with w excluded, can be regarded as symbolizing the business demand for money and, as it stands, symbolizing aggregate demand for money, although with even more serious qualifications about the ambiguities introduced by aggregation.

5. The Keynesian Challenge to the Quantity Theory

The income-expenditure analysis developed by John Maynard Keynes in his *General Theory* (Keynes 1936) offered an alternative approach to the interpretation of changes in nominal income that emphasized the relation between nominal income and investment or autonomous expenditures rather than the relation between money income and the stock of money.

Keynes's basic challenge to the reigning theory can be summarized in three propositions that he set forth:

1. As a purely *theoretical* matter, there need not exist, even if all prices are flexible, a *long-run equilibrium* position characterized by "full employment" of resources.

2. As an *empirical* matter, prices can be regarded as rigid—an institutional datum—for *short-run economic fluctuations;* that is, for such fluctuations, the distinction between real and nominal magnitudes that is at the heart of the quantity theory is of no importance.

3. The demand function for money has a particular empirical form —corresponding to absolute liquidity preference—that makes velocity highly unstable much of the time, so that changes in the quantity of money would, in the main, simply produce changes in V in the opposite direction. This proposition is critical for both propositions (1) and (2), though the reasons for absolute liquidity preference are different in the long run and in the short run. Absolute liquidity preference at an interest rate approaching zero is a necessary though not a sufficient condition for proposition (1). Absolute liquidity preference at the "conventional" interest rate explains why Keynes regarded the quantity equation, though perfectly valid as an identity, as largely useless for policy or for predicting short-run fluctuations in nominal and real income (identical by proposition [2]). In its place, Keynes put the income identity supplemented by a stable propensity to consume.

a) Long-Run Equilibrium

The first proposition can be treated summarily because it has been demonstrated to be false. Keynes's error consisted in neglecting the role of wealth in the consumption function—or, stated differently, in neglecting the existence of a desired stock of wealth as a goal motivating savings.[5] All sorts of frictions and rigidities may interfere with the attainment of a hypothetical long-run equilibrium position at full employment; dynamic changes in technology, resources, and social and economic institutions may continually change the characteristics of that equilibrium position; but there is no fundamental "flaw in the price system" that makes unemployment the natural outcome of a fully operative market mechanism.[6]

b) Short-Run Price Rigidity[7]

Alfred Marshall's distinction among market equilibrium, short-period equilibrium, and long-period equilibrium was a device for analyzing

[5] Keynes, of course, verbally recognized this point, but it was not incorporated in his formal model of the economy. Its key role was pointed out first by Haberler (1941, pp. 242, 389, 403, 491–503) and subsequently by Pigou (1947), Tobin (1947), Patinkin (1951), and Johnson (1961).

[6] This proposition played a large role in gaining for Keynes the adherence of many noneconomists, particularly the large band of reformers, social critics, and radicals who were persuaded that there was something fundamentally wrong with the capitalist "system." There is a long history of attempts, some highly sophisticated, to demonstrate that there is a "flaw in the price system" (the title of one such attempt [Martin 1924]), attempts going back at least to Malthus. In modern times, one of the most popular and persistent is the "social credit" doctrine of Major C. H. Douglas, which even spawned a political party in Canada that captured control (in 1935) of the government of one of the Canadian provinces (Alberta) and attempted to implement some of Major Douglas's doctrines. This policy ran into legal obstacles and had to be abandoned. The successor party now (1969) controls Alberta and British Columbia. But, prior to Keynes, these attempts had been made primarily by persons outside of the mainstream of the economics profession, and professional economists had little trouble in demonstrating their theoretical flaws and inadequacies.

Keynes's attempt was therefore greeted with enthusiasm. It came from a professional economist of the very highest repute, regarded, and properly so, by his fellow economists as one of the great economists of all time. The analytical system was sophisticated and complex, yet, once mastered, appeared highly mechanical and capable of yielding far-reaching and important conclusions with a minimum of input; and these conclusions were, besides, highly congenial to the opponents of the market system.

Needless to say, the demonstration that this proposition of Keynes's is false, and even the acceptance of this demonstration by economists who regard themselves as disciples of the Keynes of *The General Theory,* has not prevented the noneconomist opponents of the market system from continuing to believe that Keynes proved the proposition, and continuing to cite his authority for it.

[7] We are indebted to a brilliant book by Leijonhufvud (1968) for a full ap-

the dynamic adjustment in a particular market to a change in demand or supply. This device had two key characteristics. One, the less important for our purposes, is that it replaced the continuous process by a series of discrete steps—comparable with approximating a continuous function by a set of straight-line segments. The second is the assumption that prices adjust more rapidly than quantities, indeed, so rapidly that the price adjustment can be regarded as instantaneous. An increase in demand (a shift to the right of the long-run demand curve) will produce a new market equilibrium involving a higher price but the same quantity. The higher price will, in the short run, encourage existing producers to produce more with their existing plants, thus raising quantity and bringing prices back down toward their original level, and, in the long run, attract new producers and encourage existing producers to expand their plants, still further raising quantities and lowering prices. Throughout the process, it takes time for output to adjust but no time for prices to do so. This assumption has no effect on the final equilibrium position, but it is vital for the path to equilibrium.

This Marshallian assumption about the price of a particular product became widely accepted and tended to be carried over unthinkingly to the price level in analyzing the dynamic adjustment to a change in the demand for or supply of money. As noted above, the Cambridge cash-balances equation lends itself to a demand-supply interpretation along Marshallian lines (Pigou 1917). So interpreted, a change in the nominal quantity of money (a once-for-all shift in the supply schedule) will require a change in one or more of the variables on the right-hand side of equation (6)—k, or P, or y—in order to reconcile demand and supply. In the final full equilibrium, the adjustment will, in general, be entirely in P, since the change in the nominal quantity of money need not alter any of the "real" factors on which k and y ultimately depend.[8] As in the Marshallian case, the final position is not affected by relative speeds of adjustment.

There is nothing in the logic of the quantity theory that specifies the dynamic path of adjustment, nothing that requires the whole adjustment to take place through P rather than through k or y. It was widely recog-

---

preciation of the importance of this proposition in Keynes's system. This subsection and the one that follows, on the liquidity preference function, owe much to Leijonhufvud's penetrating analysis.

[8] The "in general" is inserted to warn the reader that this is a complex question, requiring for a full analysis a much more careful statement of just how the quantity of money is increased. However, these more sophisticated issues are not relevant to the point under discussion and so are bypassed.

nized that the adjustment during what Fisher, for example, called "transition periods" would in practice be partly in k and in y as well as in P. Yet this recognition was not incorporated in formal theoretical analysis. The formal analysis simply took over Marshall's assumption. In this sense, the quantity theorists can be validly criticized for having "assumed" price flexibility—just as Keynes can be validly criticized for "assuming" that consumption is independent of wealth, even though he recognized in his asides that wealth has an effect on consumption.

Keynes was a true Marshallian in method. He followed Marshall in taking the demand-supply analysis as his framework. He followed Marshall in replacing the continuous adjustment by a series of discrete steps and so analyzing a dynamic process in terms of a series of shifts between static equilibrium positions. Even his steps were essentially Marshall's, his short-run being distinguished from his long-run by the fixity of the aggregate capital stock. However, he tended to merge the market period and the short-run period, and, true to his own misleading dictum, "in the long run we are all dead," he concentrated almost exclusively on the short run.

Keynes also followed Marshall in assuming that one variable adjusted so quickly that the adjustment could be regarded as instantaneous, while the other variable adjusted slowly. Where he deviated from Marshall, and it was a momentous deviation, was in reversing the roles assigned to price and quantity. He assumed that, at least for changes in aggregate demand, quantity was the variable that adjusted rapidly, while price was the variable that adjusted slowly,[9] at least in a downward direction. Keynes embodied this assumption in his formal model by expressing all variables in wage units, so that his formal analysis— aside from a few passing references to a situation of "true" inflation— dealt with "real" magnitudes, not "nominal" magnitudes (Keynes 1936, pp. 119, 301, 303). He rationalized the assumption in terms of wage rigidity arising partly from money illusion, partly from the strength of trade unions. And, at a still deeper level, he rationalized wage rigidity by proposition (1): under conditions when there was no full-employment equilibrium, there was also no equilibrium nominal price level; something had to be brought in from outside to fix the price level; it might as well be institutional wage rigidity. Put differ-

---

[9] I have referred to "quantity," not "output," because I conjecture that Keynes, if pressed to distinguish the market from the short-run period, would have done so by regarding quantity available to purchase as adjusting rapidly in the market period largely through changes in inventories, and in the short-run period through changes in output.

ently, flexible nominal wages under such circumstances had no economic function to perform; hence they might as well be made rigid.

However rationalized, the basic reason for the assumption was undoubtedly the lack of concordance between observed phenomena and the implications of a literal application of Marshall's assumption to aggregate magnitudes. Such a literal application implied that economic fluctuations would take the form wholly of fluctuations in prices with continuous full employment of men and resources. Clearly, this did not correspond to experience. If anything, at least in the decade and a half between the end of World War I and the writing of *The General Theory*, economic fluctuations were manifested to a greater degree in output and employment than in prices. It therefore seemed highly plausible that, at least for aggregate phenomena, relative speeds of adjustment were just the reverse of those assumed by Marshall.[10]

Keynes explored this penetrating insight by carrying it to the extreme: all adjustment in quantity, none in price. He qualified this statement by assuming it to apply only to conditions of underemployment. At "full" employment, he shifted to the quantity-theory model and asserted that all adjustment would be in price—he designated this a situation of "true inflation." However, Keynes paid no more than lip service to this possibility, and his disciples have done the same; so it does not misrepresent the body of his analysis largely to neglect the qualification.

Given this assumption, a change in the nominal quantity of money means a change in the real quantity of money. In equation (6) we can divide through by P, making the left-hand side the real quantity of money. A change in the (nominal and real) quantity of money will then be matched by a change in k or in y.

Nothing up to this point seems to prevent Keynes from having a purely monetary theory of economic fluctuations, with changes in M being reflected entirely in y. However, this conflicted with Keynes's interpretation of the facts of the Great Depression, which he regarded, I believe erroneously, as showing that expansive monetary policy was ineffective in stemming a decline (Friedman 1967). Hence, he was inclined to interpret changes in M as being reflected in k rather more

---

[10] I do not mean to suggest that Marshall's assumption is always the best one for particular markets. On the contrary, one of the significant advances in recent years in relative price theory is the development of more sophisticated price adjustment models that allow the rates of adjustment of both price and quantity to vary continuously between instantaneous and very slow adjustment. However, these developments are not directly relevant to the present discussion, although they partly inspire section 12 below.

than in y. This is where his proposition (3) about liquidity preference enters in.

Indeed, in the most extreme, and I am tempted to say purest, form of his analysis, Keynes supposes that the whole of the adjustment will be in k. And, interestingly enough, this result can also be regarded as a direct consequence of his assumption about the relative speed of adjustment of price and quantity. For k is not a numerical constant but a function of other variables. It embodies liquidity preference. In Keynes's system, the main variable it depends on is the interest rate. This too is a price. Hence, it was natural for Keynes to regard it as slow to adjust, and to take, as the variable which responds, the real quantity of money people desire to hold.

If changes in M do not produce changes in y, what does? Keynes's answer is the need to reconcile the amount some people want to spend to add to the stock of productive capital with the amount the community wants to save to add to its stock of wealth. Hence Keynes puts at the center of his analysis the distinction between consumption and saving, or more fundamentally, between spending linked closely to current income and spending that is largely independent of current income.

As a result of both experience and further theoretical analysis, there is hardly an economist today who accepts Keynes's conclusion about the strictly passive character of k, or the accompanying conclusion that money (in the sense of the quantity of money) does not matter, or who will explicitly assert that P is "really" an institutional datum that will be completely unaffected even in short periods by changes in M (Friedman 1968, 1970b).

Yet Keynes's assumption about the relative speed of adjustment of price and quantity is still a key to the difference in approach and analysis between those economists who regard themselves as Keynesians and those who do not. Whatever the first group may say in their asides and in their qualifications, they treat the price level as an institutional datum in their formal theoretical analysis. They continue to regard changes in the nominal quantity of money as equivalent to changes in the real quantity of money and hence as having to be reflected in k and y. And they continue to regard the initial effect as being on k. The difference is that they no longer regard interest rates as institutional data, as Keynes in considerable measure did. Instead, they regard the change in k as requiring a change in interest rates which in turn produces a change in y. Hence, they attribute more significance to changes in the quantity of money than Keynes and his disciples did in the first decade or so after the appearance of The General Theory.

A striking illustration is provided in a recent Cowles Foundation Monograph, edited by Donald Hester and James Tobin, on *Financial Markets and Economic Activity* (Hester and Tobin 1967). A key essay in that book presents a comparative static analysis of the general equilibrium adjustment of stocks of assets. Yet the distinction between nominal and real magnitudes is not even discussed. The entire analysis is valid only on the implicit assumption that nominal prices of goods and services are completely rigid, although interest rates and real magnitudes are flexible.[11]

The National Bureau series of monetary studies illustrates the other side of the coin—the approach of those of us who do not regard ourselves as Keynesians. Many of the questions discussed in these monographs would not have appeared to be open questions, and large parts of them would never have been written, had we, implicitly or explicitly, accepted Keynes's assumption that prices are an institutional datum.

c) *Absolute Liquidity Preference*

Keynes gave a highly specific form to equation (6) or (7). The quantity of money demanded, he argued, could be treated as if it were divided

---

[11] See Tobin and Brainard (1967). A specific example documenting this statement is that Tobin and Brainard explicitly assume that central banks can determine the ratio of currency (or high-powered money) to total wealth including real assets (Hester and Tobin 1967, pp. 61–62). If prices are flexible, the central bank can determine only nominal magnitudes, not such a real ratio.

Other papers in Monograph 21, notably the paper by Brainard, "Financial Institutions and a Theory of Monetary Control" (Brainard 1967), make the same implicit assumptions. The word "prices" does not appear in the cumulative subject index of this monograph and of two companion volumes, Monographs 19 and 20.

Still another more recent example is a paper by the same authors, "Pitfalls in Financial Model Building" (Tobin and Brainard 1968), in which they present a simulation of a "fictitious economy of our construction." In this economy, the replacement value of physical assets is used as the numeraire of the system, and all prices are expressed relative to the replacement value. The result is that the system—intended to illuminate the problems of monetary analysis—takes the absolute price level as determined outside the system. The Central Bank is implicitly assumed to be able to determine the *real* and not merely the *nominal* volume of bank reserves.

Another striking example is Gramley and Chase (1965). In this article, the assumption about price rigidity is explicit and presented as if it were only a tentative assumption made for convenience of analysis. Yet the empirical significance Gramley and Chase attach to their results belies this profession.

See also the econometric study by Goldfeld (1966), which concentrates on real forms of the functions estimated because of "the superiority of the deflated version" (p. 166).

Evidence for a somewhat earlier period is provided by Holzman and Bronfenbrenner (1963). Theories of inflation stemming from the Keynesian approach stress institutional, not monetary, factors.

into two parts, one part, M_1, "held to satisfy the transactions- and precautionary-motives," the other, M_2, "held to satisfy the speculative-motive" (Keynes 1936, p. 199). He regarded M_1 as a roughly constant fraction of income. He regarded the (short-run) demand for M_2 as arising from *"uncertainty* as to the future of the rate of interest" and the amount demanded as depending on the relation between current rates of interest and the rates of interest expected to prevail in the future (Keynes 1936, p. 168; italics in original). Keynes, of course, emphasized that there was a whole complex of interest rates. However, for simplicity, he spoke in terms of "the rate of interest," usually meaning by that the rate on long-term securities that involved minimal risks of default—for example, government bonds. The key distinction to Keynes was between short-term and long-term securities, not between securities fixed in nominal value and those that were not. The latter distinction was rendered irrelevant by his assumption that prices were rigid.

The distinction between short-term and long-term securities was important to Keynes because it corresponded to differences in risk of capital gain or loss as a result of changes in interest rates. For short-term securities, changes in interest rates would have little effect. For long-term securities, the effect is important. Leijonhufvud has argued, and we believe correctly, that Keynes used the term "money" as referring not only to currency and deposits narrowly defined but to the whole range of short-term assets that provided "liquidity" in the sense of security against capital loss arising from changes in interest rates.[12] Needless to say, Keynes also regarded other kinds of risks, such as risks of default, as highly relevant, but, consistent with his proposition (2), he almost entirely disregarded risks arising from changes in the price level of goods and services (Leijonhufvud 1968, chap. 2).

It is therefore somewhat misleading to regard Keynes, as most of the literature does, as distinguishing between "money" and "bonds." Nonetheless, we shall continue to follow current practice and use that terminology. One justification for doing so is that Keynes did treat the short-term assets he labeled "money" as yielding no interest return. (It is well to recall that he was writing at a time when short-term interest rates were extremely low both absolutely and relative to long-term rates. His procedure would seem highly unrealistic today.)

---

[12] In this respect, the Radcliffe Committee is faithful to Keynes in treating "liquidity" broadly defined as the relevant monetary aggregate rather than "money" narrowly defined.

To formalize Keynes's analysis in terms of the symbols we have used so far, we can write his demand function as

$$\frac{M}{P} = \frac{M_1}{P} + \frac{M_2}{P} = k_1 y + f(r - r^*, r^*), \qquad (8)$$

where r is the current rate of interest, r^* is the rate of interest expected to prevail, and k_1, the analogue to the inverse of income velocity of circulation of money, is treated as determined by payment practices and hence as a constant at least in the short run.[13] The current interest rate, r, is an observed magnitude. Hence it will be the same for all holders of money, if, like Keynes, we abstract from the existence of a complex of interest rates. The expected rate, r^*, is not observable. It may differ from one holder to another and, for each holder separately, is to be interpreted as the mean value of a probability distribution, not as a single value anticipated with certainty. For an aggregate function, r^* should strictly speaking be interpreted as a vector, not a number. Though I have introduced P into the equation for consistency with my earlier equations, Keynes omitted it because of his proposition (2), which meant that P, or, more precisely, the wage rate, was taken to be a constant.

In a "given state of expectations," that is, for a given value of r^*, the higher is the current rate of interest, the lower will be the amount of money people would want to hold for speculative motives. The cost of holding money instead of securities would be greater in two ways: first, a larger amount of current earnings would be sacrificed; second, it would be more likely that interest rates would fall, and hence security prices rise, and so a larger amount of capital gains would be sacrificed.

Although expectations are given great prominence in developing the liquidity function expressing the demand for M_2, Keynes and his followers generally did not explicitly introduce them, as I have done, into that function. For the most part, Keynes and his followers in practice treated the amount of M_2 demanded simply as a function of the current interest rate, the emphasis on expectations serving only as a reason for their attribution of instability to the liquidity function.[14]

The reason for this omission is their concentration on the short-run demand function. For that function, they regarded r^* as fixed, so that the speculative demand was a function of r alone. I have introduced

---

[13] Later writers in this tradition have argued that k_1 too should be regarded as a function of interest rates. See Baumol (1952), and Tobin (1956). However, this issue is not relevant to the present discussion.

[14] A notable exception is Tobin (1958, pp. 65–86).

r^* in order to distinguish between the different reasons that are implicit in Keynes's analysis for absolute liquidity preference in the short run and the long run.

Keynes's special twist was less expressing the demand function in the general form described by equation (8) than the particular form he gave to the function $f(r - r^*, r^*)$. For given r^*, he believed that this function would be highly elastic at $r = r^*$, the degree of elasticity at an observed numerical value of r depending on how homogenous the expectations of different holders of money are and how firmly they are held.[15] Let there be a substantial body of holders of money who have the same expectation and who hold that expectation firmly, and f will become perfectly elastic at that current interest rate. Money and bonds would become perfect substitutes; liquidity preference would become absolute. The monetary authorities would find it impossible to change the interest rate because speculators holding these firm expectations would frustrate them.

Under such circumstances, if the monetary authorities sought to increase the amount of money by buying bonds, this would tend to raise bond prices and lower the rate of return on bonds. Even the slightest lowering would, Keynes argued, lead speculators with firm expectations to absorb the additional money balances and sell the bonds demanded by the holders of money. The result would simply be that the community as a whole would be willing to hold the increased quantity of money; k would be higher and V lower. Conversely, if the monetary authorities decreased the amount of money by selling bonds, this would tend to raise the rate of interest, and even the slightest rise would induce the speculators to absorb the bonds offered. (In Keynes's analysis, the result would be the same if the amount of money were increased or decreased by operations that added to or subtracted from total wealth, rather than by substituting one form of wealth for another, because he assumed that wealth had no direct effect on spending.)

Or, again, suppose there is an increase in nominal income for whatever reason. That will require an increase in M_1, which can come out of M_2 without any further effects. Conversely, any decline in M_1 can be added to M_2 without any further effects. The conclusion is that *under circumstances of absolute liquidity preference* income can change without a change in M or in interest rates and M can change without

[15] Tobin (1958) presents an excellent and illuminating analysis of this case. Because he assumes that shifts into or out of securities involve commitments for a finite period equal to the unit of time in terms of which the interest rate is expressed, his critical value is not $r = r^*$ but $r = r^*/(1 + r^*)$, current income on the securities compensating for an expected capital loss.

a change in income or in interest rates. The holders of money are in metastable equilibrium, like a tumbler on its side on a flat surface; they will be satisfied with whatever the amount of money happens to be.

For the long-run demand schedule, the reason for liquidity preference is different. In long-run equilibrium, r must equal r^*, so $f(r - r^*, r^*)$ reduces to a function of r^* alone. Let there be a deficiency of investment opportunities, the kind of situation envisaged in Keynes's proposition (1), so that r^* becomes very low. The lower the rate, the lower the return from capital assets other than money—whether these be bonds, equities, or physical assets (recall that because of the assumption that the price level is rigid, Keynes did not regard the distinction among these as important). Accordingly, the lower r^*, the lower the cost of holding money. At a sufficiently low, yet finite rate, the extra return from holding nonmoney assets would only just compensate for the extra risks involved. Hence at that rate, liquidity preference would be absolute. The "market rate" of interest could not be indefinitely low; a bottom limit was set by the widespread desire to substitute money for other assets at low interest rates.

This conclusion was a key element in Keynes's proposition (1). One way to summarize his argument for that proposition is in terms of a possible conflict between the "market" and the "equilibrium" rate of interest. If investment opportunities were sparse, yet the public's desire to save were strong, the "equilibrium" rate of interest, he argued, might have to be very low or even negative to equate investment and saving. But there was a floor to the "market rate" set by liquidity preference. If this floor exceeded the "equilibrium rate," he argued, there was a conflict that could only be resolved by unemployment that frustrated the public's thriftiness. The fallacy in this argument is that the introduction of money not only introduces a floor to the "market rate"; it also sets a floor to the "equilibrium rate." And, in the long run, the two floors are identical. This is the essence of the so-called Pigou effect (Friedman 1962, pp. 262–63).

Neither Keynes himself, nor most of his disciples and followers, distinguished as sharply as I have between the short-run and long-run liquidity traps. They tended to merge the two and, in line with the general emphasis on the short run, to stress elasticity with respect to current, not expected, interest rates.[16]

Keynes regarded absolute liquidity preference as a strictly "limiting case" of which, though it "might become practically important in

---

[16] Tobin makes an explicit distinction of this kind, though not in connection with a liquidity trap as such.

future," he knew "of no example . . . hitherto" (Keynes 1936, p. 207). However, he treated velocity as if in practice its behavior frequently approximated that which would prevail in this limiting case.

Absolute liquidity preference is no longer explicitly avowed by today's economists—the failure of central banks in their attempts to peg interest rates at low levels have made that proposition untenable. Yet, like absolutely rigid prices, it still plays an important role in the theorizing of many an economist. It is implicit in the tendency to regard k or velocity as passively adjusting to changes in the quantity of money. It is explicit in the tendency to regard the demand for money as "highly" elastic with respect to interest rates.

Consider again equation (6). Let there be a change in M. Economists in the Keynesian tradition continue, as noted earlier, to regard P as an institutional datum and so unaffected. They must therefore regard the change in M as affecting either k or y or both. With absolute liquidity preference, k can absorb the impact without any change in the interest rate. Since they take the interest rate as the only link between monetary change and real income, the whole of the change would then be absorbed in k with no effect on y. If liquidity preference is not absolute, k can change only through a change in the interest rate. But this has effects on y through investment spending. The more elastic is the demand for money, the less interest rates will have to change. The more inelastic are investment spending and saving with respect to the interest rate, the less will any given change in the interest rate affect y. Hence the tendency for these economists to regard k as absorbing the main impact of changes in M means that implicitly or explicitly they regard the demand for money as highly elastic with respect to the interest rate and investment spending and saving as highly inelastic.

The tendency on the part of many economists to assume implicitly that prices are an institutional datum and that the demand for money is highly elastic with respect to the interest rate underlies some of the criticisms that have been directed against earlier work by myself and associates. We have been interpreted, wrongly, we believe, as saying that k is completely independent of interest rates (Friedman 1966). In that case, changes in M need not be reflected at all in k. If, also, P is taken as an institutional datum, all of the effect will be on y. This is the implicit source of the criticism leveled against us, that we regard the quantity of money as determining the level of economic activity. Not only, say our critics, do we believe that money matters, we believe that money is all that matters (Okun 1963; Tobin 1965a, p. 481).

If P is not regarded as an institutional datum, and we have not so regarded it, then even if we supposed k to be completely insensitive to interest rates and to anything else that might be affected by changes in M (such as the rate of change in P or in y) and so to be an absolute constant, aside from random disturbances, something other than the quantity of money would have to be brought into the analysis to explain how much of the change in M would be reflected in P and how much in y (see section 12, below).

We have always tried to qualify our statements about the importance of changes in M by referring to their effect on *nominal* income. But this qualification appeared meaningless to economists who implicitly identified nominal with real magnitudes. Hence they have misunderstood our conclusions.

We have accepted the quantity-theory presumption, and have thought it supported by the evidence we examined, that changes in the quantity of money as such *in the long run* have a negligible effect on real income, so that nonmonetary forces are "all that matter" for changes in real income over the decades and money "does not matter." On the other hand, we have regarded the quantity of money, plus the other variables (including real income itself) that affect k as essentially "all that matter" for the long-run determination of nominal income. The price level is then a joint outcome of the monetary forces determining nominal income and the real forces determining real income (Friedman 1958, pp. 242–46; Friedman and Schwartz 1963*b*, p. 695).

For shorter periods of time, we have argued that changes in M will be reflected in all three variables on the right-hand side of equation (6): k, P, and y. But we have argued that the effect on k is empirically not to absorb the change in M, as the Keynesian analysis implies, but often to reinforce it, changes in M and k frequently affecting income in the same rather than opposite directions. Hence we have emphasized that changes in M are a major factor, though even then not the only factor, accounting for short-run changes in both nominal income and the real level of activity (y). I regard the description of our position as "money is all that matters for changes in *nominal* income and for *short-run* changes in real income" as an exaggeration but one that gives the right flavor of our conclusions. I regard the statement that "money is all that matters," period, as a basic misrepresentation of our conclusions (Friedman 1958, pp. 246–51; Friedman and Schwartz 1963*a*, pp. 38–39, 45–46, 55–64; Friedman and Schwartz 1963*b*, p. 678).

Another, more subtle, difference between the approach of the economists in the Keynesian tradition and the approach that we have adopted has also contributed to much misunderstanding. This difference is in the transmission mechanism that is assumed to connect a change in the quantity of money with a change in total nominal income (= total spending). The Keynesians regard a change in the quantity of money as affecting in the first instance "the" interest rate, interpreted as a market rate on a fairly narrow class of financial liabilities. They regard spending as affected only "indirectly" as the changed interest rate alters the profitability and amount of investment spending, again interpreted fairly narrowly, and as investment spending, through the multiplier, affects total spending. Hence the emphasis they give in their analysis to the interest elasticities of the demand for money and of investment spending. We, on the other hand, stress a much broader and more "direct" impact on spending, saying, as in section 1 above, that individuals seeking "to dispose of what they regard as their excess money balances . . . will try to pay out a larger sum for the purchase of securities, goods and services, for the repayment of debts, and as gifts than they are receiving from the corresponding sources."

The two approaches can be readily reconciled on a formal level. The transmission mechanism that we have stressed can be described as operating "through" the balance sheet and "through" changes in interest rates. The attempt by holders of money to restore or attain a desired balance sheet after an unexpected increase in the quantity of money will tend to raise the prices of assets and reduce interest rates, which will encourage both spending to produce new assets and spending on current services rather than on purchasing existing assets. This is how an initial effect on balance sheets gets translated into an effect on income and spending.

The difference between us and the Keynesians is less in the nature of the process than in the range of assets considered. The Keynesians tend to concentrate on a narrow range of marketable assets and recorded interest rates. We insist that a far wider range of assets and interest rates must be taken into account—such assets as durable and semi-durable consumer goods, structures and other real property. As a result, we regard the market rates stressed by the Keynesians as only a small part of the total spectrum of rates that are relevant (Friedman 1961, pp. 461–463; Friedman and Meiselman 1963, pp. 217–222; Friedman and Schwartz 1963a, pp. 59-63; Friedman 1970b, pp. 24–25; Brunner 1970, pp. 3–5).

This difference in the assumed transmission mechanism is largely a by-product of the different assumptions about price. The rejection of absolute liquidity preference forced Keynes's followers to let the interest rate be flexible. This chink in the key assumption that prices are an institutional datum was minimized by interpreting the "interest rate" narrowly, and market institutions made it easy to do so. After all, it is most unusual to quote houses, automobiles, let alone furniture, household appliances, clothes and so on, in terms of the "interest rate" implicit in their sales and rental prices. Hence the prices of these items continued to be regarded as an institutional datum, which forced the transmission process to go through an extremely narrow channel. On our side, there was no such inhibition. Since we regarded prices as flexible, though not "perfectly" flexible, it was natural for us to interpret the transmission mechanism in terms of relative price adjustments over a broad area rather than in terms of narrowly defined interest rates.

6. A Simple Common Model

We can summarize the key points of the preceding sections of this paper, and lay a groundwork for the final sections, by setting forth a highly simplified aggregate model of an economy that encompasses both a simplified quantity theory and a simplified income-expenditure theory as special cases. In interpreting this model, it should be kept in mind that the same symbols can have very different empirical counterparts, so that the algebraic statement can conceal a difference as fundamental as that described in the preceding four paragraphs.

For the purpose of this summary, we can neglect foreign trade, by assuming a closed economy, and the fiscal role of government, by assuming that there are neither government expenditures nor government receipts. We can also neglect stochastic disturbances. What I shall concentrate on are the division of national income between induced and autonomous expenditures and the adjustment between the demand for and supply of money.

The simple model is given by six equations:

$$\frac{C}{P} = f\left(\frac{Y}{P}, r\right); \tag{9}$$

$$\frac{I}{P} = g(r); \tag{10}$$

$$\frac{Y}{P} = \frac{C}{P} + \frac{I}{P} \text{ (or, alternatively, } \frac{S}{P} = \frac{Y-C}{P} = \frac{I}{P}); \tag{11}$$

$$M^D = P \cdot l\left(\frac{Y}{P}, r\right); \tag{12}$$

$$M^S = h(r); \tag{13}$$

$$M^D = M^S. \tag{14}$$

The first three equations describe the adjustment of the flows of savings and investment; the last three, of the stock of money demanded and supplied. Equation (9) is a consumption function (Keynes's "marginal propensity to consume") expressing real consumption (C/P) as a function of real income $(Y/P = y)$ and the interest rate (r). For simplicity, wealth is omitted, although, if the model were to be used to illustrate Keynes's proposition (1), and why it is fallacious, wealth would have to be included as an argument in the function.

Equation (10) is an investment function (Keynes's marginal efficiency of investment) which expresses real investment (I/P) as a function of the interest rate. Here again, consistent with both Keynes and subsequent literature, both the total stock of capital and real income could be included as arguments. However, in Keynes's spirit, the model refers to a short period in which the capital stock can be regarded as fixed. For a longer-period model, the capital stock would have to be included and treated as an endogenous variable, presumably defined by an integral of past investment. The inclusion of income in the equation, as an independent variable, would confuse the key point of the distinction between C and I. As a theoretical matter, the relevant distinction is not between consumption and investment but between expenditures that are closely linked to current income ("conditional" on income would, from this point of view, be a better mnemonic for C than consumption, though the term usually used is "induced") and expenditures that are autonomous, that is, independent (a better mnemonic for I than investment), of income. The identification of these categories with consumption and investment is an empirical hypothesis. For theoretical purposes, any part of investment spending that is conditional on current income should be included with C.

Equation (11) is typically referred to as the income identity. As the parenthetical transformation makes clear, it can also be regarded as a market-clearing or adjustment equation specifying that saving is to be equal to investment.

Equation (12) is the demand function for nominal money balances (Keynes's liquidity preference function). It is simply equation (6) or (7) rewritten in simplified form and expresses the real quantity of money demanded (M^D/P) as a function of real income and the interest rate. Here again, as in equation (9), wealth could properly be included but is omitted for simplicity.

Equation (13) is the supply function of nominal money. To be consistent with the literature, the interest rate enters as a variable. However, no purpose for which we shall use the model would be affected in any way by treating M^S as simply an exogenous variable, determined, say, by the monetary authorities.[17]

Equation (14) is the counterpart of equation (11), a market-clearing or adjustment equation specifying that money demanded shall equal money supplied.

These six equations would be accepted alike by adherents of the quantity theory and of the income-expenditure theory. On this level of abstraction, there is no difference between them. However, while there are six equations, there are seven unknowns: C, I, Y, r, P, M^D, M^S. There is a missing equation. Some one of these variables must be determined by relationships outside this system.[18]

7. The Missing Equation: Three Approaches

The difference between the quantity theory and the income-expenditure theory is the condition that is added to make the equations determinate.

The simple income-expenditure theory adds the missing equation in one form. Different versions of the quantity theory add it in two other forms. Of these, the missing equation that has been generally regarded in the literature as defining the simple quantity theory is discussed in this section. The missing equation supplied by an alternative version of the quantity theory that is implicit in much recent literature but has not heretofore been made explicit is discussed in the following section. I shall designate the alternative version of the quantity theory as the monetary theory of nominal income.

The simple quantity theory adds the equation

$$\frac{Y}{P} = y = y_0; \qquad (15)$$

that is, real income is determined outside the system. In effect, it appends to this system the Walrasian equations of general equilibrium, regards

[17] This would be consistent with Cagan's findings about the absence of any significant effect of changes in the interest rate on the supply of money. However, to be consistent with his findings, income or some other indicator of business cycles would have to be included as a variable, as has been done in some empirical studies of the supply of money. See Cagan (1965, pp. 150, 228–32) and Hendershott (1968).

[18] Of course, this is speaking figuratively. It is not necessary that a single variable be so determined. What is required is an independent relation connecting some subset of the seven endogenous variables with exogenous variables, and that subset could in principle consist of all seven variables.

them as independent of these equations defining the aggregates, and as giving the value of Y/P, and thereby reduces this system to one of six equations determining six unknowns.[19]

The simple income-expenditure theory adds the equation[20]

$$P = P_0; \tag{16}$$

that is, the price level is determined outside the system, which again reduces the system to one of six equations in six unknowns. It appends to this system a historical set of prices and an institutional structure that is assumed either to keep prices rigid or to determine changes in prices on the basis of "bargaining power" or some similar set of forces. Initially, the set of forces determining prices was treated as not being incorporated in any formal body of economic analysis. More recently, the developments symbolized by the "Phillips curve" reflect attempts to bring the determination of prices back into the body of economic analysis, to establish a link between real magnitudes and the rate at which prices change from their initial historically determined level (Phillips 1958).

For the quantity theory specialization, given that $Y/P = y_0$, equations (9), (10), and (11) become a self-contained set of three equation in three unknowns: C/P, I/P, and r. Substituting (9) and (10) into (11), we have

$$y_0 - f(y_0, r) = g(r), \tag{17}$$

or a single equation which determines r. Let r_0 be this value of r. From equation (13), this determines the value of M, say M_0 which, using equation (14), converts equation (12) into

$$M_0 = P \cdot l(y_0, r_0), \tag{18}$$

which now determines P.

[19] This is the essence of what has been called the classical dichotomy. Strictly speaking, the division between consumption and investment and the rates of exchange between current and future goods or services (the set of "real" or "own" interest rates) are also determined in a Walrasian "real" system, one which admits of growth, which is why quantity theorists have tended to concentrate only on equations (12), (13), and (14). On this view, equations (9), (10), and (11) are a summarization or aggregation or subset of the Walrasian system.

[20] Keynes distinguished between the price level of products and the wage rate and allowed for a change in the ratio of the one to the other as output changed, even before the point of full employment. However, this change in relative prices plays no important role in the aspects of his theory that are relevant to our purpose, so I have simplified the model by taking prices rather than wages as rigid—a simplification that has been widely used. However, explicit reference to this simplification should have been made in an earlier paper (Friedman 1970). I am indebted to an unpublished paper by Paul Davidson for recognition that the earlier exposition on this point may have been misleading.

Equation (18) is simply the classical quantity equation, as can be seen by multiplying and dividing the right-hand side by y_0 and replacing $l(y_0, r_0)/y_0$ by its equivalent, $1/V$. If we drop the subscripts, this gives,

$$M = \frac{Py}{V},\tag{19}$$

or

$$P = \frac{MV}{y}.\tag{20}$$

For the income-expenditure specialization, setting $P = P_0$ does not in general permit of a sequential solution. Substituting equations (9) and (10) into equation (11) gives

$$\frac{Y}{P_0} - f\left(\frac{Y}{P_0}, r\right) = g(r),\tag{21}$$

an equation in two variables, Y and r. This is the *IS* curve of Hicks's famous *IS–LM* analysis (Hicks 1937). Substituting equations (12) and (13) into equation (14) gives

$$h(r) = P_0 \cdot l\left(\frac{Y}{P_0}, r\right),\tag{22}$$

a second equation in the same two variables, Y and r. This is Hicks's *LM* curve. The simultaneous solution of the two determines r and Y.

Alternatively, solve equation (21) for Y as a function of r, and substitute in equation (22). This gives a single equation which determines r as a function of the demand for and supply of money. This can be regarded as the Keynesian parallel to equation (18), which determines P as a function of the demand for and supply of money.

A simpler sequential analysis, faithful to many textbook versions of the analysis and to Keynes's own simplified model, is obtained by supposing either that Y/P is not an argument in the right-hand side of equation (12) or that absolute liquidity preference holds so that equation (12) takes the special form:

$$M^D = 0 \text{ if } r > r_0\tag{12a}$$

$$M^D = \infty \text{ if } r < r_0.$$

In either of these cases, equations (12) or (12a), (13), and (14) determine the interest rate, $r = r_0$ (just as in the simple quantity approach, equations [9], [10], and [11] do); substituting the interest rate in equation (10) determines investment, say at $I = I_0$ and in equation (9) makes consumption a function solely of income, so that real income must then be determined by the requirement that it equate saving with investment.

If we approximate the function $f(Y/P, r_0)$ by a linear form, say,

$$\frac{C}{P} = C_0 + C_1 \frac{Y}{P}, \tag{23}$$

substitute equation (23) in equation (11), and solve for Y/P, we get

$$\frac{Y}{P} = \frac{C_0 + I_0}{1 - C_1}, \tag{24}$$

or the simple Keynesian multiplier equation, with $C_0 + I_0$ equalling autonomous expenditure and $1/(1 - C_1)$ equalling the multiplier.

8. The Missing Equation: The Third Approach Examined

A third form of the missing equation involves bypassing the breakdown of nominal income between real income and prices and using the quantity theory to derive a theory of nominal income rather than a theory of either prices or real income.

a) Demand for Money

As a first step, assume that the elasticity of the demand for money with respect to real income is unity. We can then write (12) in the equivalent form:

$$M^D = Y \cdot l(r), \tag{12b}$$

where the same symbol l is used to designate a different functional form. This enables us to eliminate prices and real income separately from the equations of the monetary sector.

This assumption cannot, so far as I am aware, be justified on theoretical grounds. There is no reason why the elasticity of demand for money with respect to per capita real income should not be either less than one or greater than one at any particular level of income, or why it should be the same at all levels of real income. However, much empirical evidence indicates that the income elasticity is not very different from unity. The empirical evidence seems to me to indicate that the elasticity is generally larger than unity, perhaps in the neighborhood of 1.5 to 2.0 for economies in a period of rapid economic development, and of 1.0 to 1.5 for other circumstances. Other scholars would perhaps set it lower. More important, the present theory is for short-term fluctuations during which the variation in per capita real income is fairly small. Given that the elasticity is unlikely to exceed 2.0, no great error can be introduced for such moderate variations in income by approximating it by unity.[21]

b) Savings and Investment Functions

As a second step, it is tempting to make a similar assumption for the savings and investment functions, i.e., to write:

$$C = Y \cdot f(r), \tag{9a}$$

or,

$$C = Y \cdot f(r, Y), \tag{9b}$$

and

$$I = Y \cdot g(r), \tag{10a}$$

which would eliminate any separate influence of prices and real income from the savings-investment sector also. However, this is an unattractive simplification on both theoretical and empirical grounds. Theoretically, it dismisses Keynes' central point: the distinction between expenditures that are independent of current income (autonomous expenditures) and expenditures dependent on current income (induced expenditures). Empirically, much evidence suggests that the ratio of consumption to income over short periods is not independent of the level of measured income [equation (9a)], or of the division of a change in income between prices and output [equation (9b)]. The extensive literature on the consumption function rests on this evidence.

c) Interest Rates

A more promising route is to combine a key idea of Keynes' with a key idea of Irving Fisher's.

The idea that we take over from Keynes is that the current market interest rate (r) is largely determined by the rate that is expected to prevail over a longer period (r^*) (see section 5c above) [Leijonhufvud 1968, pp. 158, 405, 411].

Carrying this idea to its limit gives:

$$r = r^*. \tag{25}$$

[21] Of course, considerations such as these can at most be suggestive. The real test of the usefulness of this, and the later assumptions, is in the success of the resulting theory in predicting the behavior of nominal income.

The idea that we take over from Fisher is the distinction between the nominal and the real rate of interest:

$$r = \rho + \left(\frac{1}{P}\frac{dP}{dt}\right), \qquad (26)$$

where ρ is the real rate of interest and $(1/P)(dP/dt)$ is the percentage change in the price level. If the terms r and $(1/P)(dP/dt)$ refer to the observed nominal interest rate and observed rate of price change, ρ is the realized real interest rate. If they refer to "permanent" or "anticipated" values, which we shall designate by attaching an asterisk to them, then ρ^* is likewise the "permanent" or "anticipated" real rate.

Combine equation (25) and the version of (26) that has asterisks attached to the variables. This gives:

$$r = \rho^* + \left(\frac{1}{P}\frac{dP}{dt}\right)^*, \qquad (27)$$

which can be written as:

$$r = \rho^* + \left(\frac{1}{Y}\frac{dY}{dt}\right)^* - \left(\frac{1}{y}\frac{dy}{dt}\right)^* = \rho^* - g^* + \left(\frac{1}{Y}\frac{dY}{dt}\right)^* \qquad (28)$$

where $g^* = [(1/y)(dy/dt)]^* =$ "permanent" or "anticipated" rate of growth of real income, i.e., the secular or trend rate of growth.

Let us now assume that

$$\rho^* - g^* = k_o, \qquad (29)$$

i.e., that the difference between the anticipated real interest rate and the anticipated rate of real growth is determined outside the system. This equation is the counterpart of the full employment and rigid price assumptions [equations (15) and (16)] of the simple quantity theory and the simple Keynesian income-expenditure theory.

There are two ways that assumption (29) can be rationalized: (1) that over a time interval relevant for the analysis of short-period fluctuations, ρ^* and g^* can separately be regarded as constant; (2) that the two can be regarded as moving together, so the difference will vary less than either. Of course, in both cases, what is relevant is not absolute constancy, but changes in $\rho^* - g^*$ that are small compared to changes in $[(1/P)(dP/dt)]^*$, and hence in r.

(1) The stock of physical capital, the stock of human capital, and the body of technological knowledge are all extremely large compared to annual additions. Physical capital is, say, of the order of three to five years' national income; annual net investment is of the order of

$\frac{1}{10}$ to $\frac{1}{5}$ of national income or 2 to 8 per cent of the capital stock. Let the capital *stock* be subject even to very rapidly diminishing returns and the real yield will not be much affected in a few years time. Similar considerations apply to human capital and technology.

If we interpret g^* as referring to growth potential, then a roughly constant yield on capital, human and nonhuman, and a slowly changing stock of capital imply a slowly changing value of g^* as well.

Empirically, a number of pieces of evidence fit in with these assumptions. We have interest rate data over very long periods of time, and these indicate that rates are very similar at distant times, if the times compared have similar price behavior (Gupta 1964). More recently, the Federal Reserve Bank of St. Louis has been estimating the "real rate," and their estimates are remarkably stable despite very large changes in nominal rates.

Similarly, average real growth has differed considerably at any one time for different countries—compare Japan in recent decades with Great Britain—but for each country has been rather constant over considerable periods of time.

(2) Let $s^* =$ the fraction of permanent income which is invested. Then the permanent rate of growth of income as a result of this investment alone will be equal to $s^* \rho^*$. Empirically, the actual rate of growth tends to be larger than this product, if s^* refers only to what is recorded as capital formation in the national income accounts. One explanation, frequently suggested, is that recorded capital formation neglects most investment in human capital and in improving technology and that allowance for these would make the relevant s^* much higher than the 10 or 20 per cent that is the fraction estimated in national income accounts, both because it would increase the numerator of the fraction (investment) and decrease the denominator (income) by requiring much of what is commonly treated as income to be treated as expenses of maintaining human capital and the stock of technology. In the limit, as s^* approaches unity, ρ^* approaches g^*, so $\rho^* - g^* = 0$.[22] Without going to this extreme,

$$\rho^* - g^* = (1 - s^*)\rho^*. \tag{30}$$

The preceding argument suggests that ρ^* is fairly constant, and subtracting g^* decreases the error even further.

---

[22] An argument justifying this equality on a purely theoretical level has been developed ingeniously and perceptively by Stephen Friedberg in some unpublished papers that take Frank H. Knight's capital theory as their starting point. This equality is also a key implication of Von Neumann's general equilibrium model (Von Neumann 1945, p. 7).

Empirically, it does seem to be the case that ρ^* and g^* tend to vary together, though in the present state of evidence, this is hardly more than a rough conjecture.

(d) The Alternative Model

If we substitute equation (12b) for equation (12), keep the original equations (13) and (14), and substitute equation (29) in equation (28) to replace the remaining equations of the initial simple model, we have the following system of four equations:

$$M^D = Y \cdot l(r) \tag{12b}$$

$$M^S = h(r) \tag{13}$$

$$M^D = M^S \tag{14}$$

$$r = k_0 + \left(\frac{1}{Y}\frac{dY}{dt}\right)^*. \tag{31}$$

At any point of time, $[(1/Y)\,(dY/dt)]^*$, the "permanent" or "anticipated" rate of growth of nominal income is a predetermined variable, presumably based partly on past experience, partly on considerations outside our model. As a result, this is a system of four equations in the four unknowns, M^D, M^S, Y, and r.

Prices and quantity do not enter separately, so the set of equations constitutes a model of nominal income.

It will help to clarify the essence of this third approach to simplify it still further by assuming that the nominal money supply can be regarded as completely exogenous, rather than a function of the interest rate,[23] and to introduce time explicitly in the system. Let $M(t)$ be the exogenously determined supply of money. We then have from equations (12b), (13), and (14)

$$Y(t) = \frac{M(t)}{l(r)}, \tag{32}$$

or

$$Y(t) = V(r) \cdot M(t), \tag{33}$$

where V stands for velocity of circulation. This puts the equation in standard quantity theory terms, except that it does not try to go behind

---

[23] Alternatively, we could write equation (13) as

$$M^S = H \cdot m(r),$$

where H is high-powered money and $m(r)$ is the money multiplier.

nominal income to prices and quantities. Equations (31) and (33) then constitute a two-equation system for determining the level of nominal income at any point in time. To determine the path of nominal income over time, there is needed in addition some way to determine the anticipated rate of change of nominal income. I shall return to this below.

Although the symbolism in the demand equation for money [(12b) or (33)] is the same as in the two other specializations of the general model, there is an important difference in substance. Both the simple quantity theory and the income-expenditure theory implicitly define equilibrium in terms of a stable price level, hence real and nominal interest rates are the same. The third approach, based on a synthesis of Keynes and Fisher, abandons this limitation. The equations encompass "equilibrium" situations in which prices may be rising or falling. The interest rate that enters into the demand schedule for money is the nominal interest rate. So long as we stick to a single interest rate, that rate takes full account of the effect of rising or falling prices on the demand for money.

(e) The Saving-Investment Sector

What about equations (9) to (11), which we have so far completely bypassed? Here the interest rate that is relevant, if a single rate is used, is clearly the real not the nominal rate. If we replace r by ρ, these equations become

$$\frac{C}{P} = f\left(\frac{Y}{P}, \rho\right) \tag{9'}$$

$$\frac{I}{P} = g(\rho) \tag{10'}$$

$$\frac{Y}{P} = \frac{C}{P} + \frac{I}{P}. \tag{11}$$

If we were to accept a more restricted counterpart of equations (25) and (29), namely

$$\rho = \rho^* = \rho_o, \tag{34}$$

i.e., the realized real rate of interest is a constant, then these equations would be a self-contained consistent set of five equations in the five variables, $C/P, I/P, Y/P, \rho, \rho^*$. Equations (34) would give the real interest rate. Equation (10)' would give real investment and equations

(9)′ and (11), real income. The price level would then be given by the ratio of the nominal income obtained from equations (31) and (33) to the real income given by equations (9)′, (10)′, (11), and (34). The two sets of equations combined would be a complete system of seven equations in seven variables determining both real and nominal magnitudes.

Such a combination, if it were acceptable, would be intellectually very appealing. Over a decade ago, during the early stages of our comparison of the predictive accuracy of the quantity theory and the income-expenditure theory, my hopes were aroused that such a combination might correspond with experience. Some of our early results were consistent with the determination of the real variables by the multiplier, and the nominal variables by velocity. However, later results shattered the hope for this outcome (Friedman and Meiselman 1963). The unfavorable empirical findings, moreover, are reinforced by theoretical considerations.

The major theoretical objections are twofold. First, it seems entirely satisfactory to take the anticipated real interest rate (or the difference between the anticipated real interest rate and the secular rate of growth) as fixed for the demand for money. There, the real interest rate is at best a supporting actor. Inflation and deflation are surely center stage. Suppressing the variations in the real interest rate (or the deviations of the measured real rate from the anticipated real rate) is unlikely to introduce serious error. The situation is altogether different for saving and investment. Omitting the real interest rate in that process is to leave out Hamlet. Second, the consumption function (9)′ is highly unsatisfactory, especially once we take inflation and deflation into account. Wealth, anticipations of inflation, and the difference between permanent and measured income are too important and too central to be pushed off stage completely.

Hence for both empirical and theoretical reasons, I am inclined to reject this way of marrying the real and the nominal variables and to regard the saving-investment sector as unfinished business, even on the highly abstract general level of this paper.

9. Some Dynamic Implications of the Monetary Theory of Nominal Income

In equation (31), which determines r, we have so far taken $[(1/Y)(dY/dt)]^*$ as a predetermined variable at time t and not looked closely at its antecedents. It is natural to regard it as determined by past history. If it is, we can write equation (33) as

$$Y(t) = V[Y(T)] \cdot M(t), \ T < t, \tag{35}$$

where V is now a functional of the past history of income, $Y(T)$ for $T < t$. However, the past history of income in its turn is a function of the past history of money, thanks to equation (33) for earlier dates. Hence, we can also write equation (33) as

$$Y(t) = F[M(T)] \cdot M(t), \ T < t, \tag{36}$$

where F is a functional of the past history of money. There is also imbedded in these equations the value k_0, i.e., the assumed fixed value of the difference between the anticipated real interest rate and the secular rate of growth of output. So equations (35) and (36) must be interpreted as depicting the movements of nominal income around a long-term trend on which k_0, and its components, ρ^* and g^*, adjust to more basic long-term forces—fundamentally for both, changes in the quantity of resources available (human and nonhuman) and in technology.

A specific example may help to bring out the dynamic character of this simple model. Take logarithms of both sides of equation (33) and differentiate with respect to time. This gives

$$\begin{aligned}
\frac{1}{Y}\frac{dY}{dt} &= \frac{1}{V}\frac{dV}{dt} + \frac{1}{M}\frac{dM}{dt} \\
&= \frac{1}{V}\frac{dV}{dr}\frac{dr}{dt} + \frac{1}{M}\frac{dM}{dt}.
\end{aligned} \tag{37}$$

Replace $(1/V)(dV/dr)$ by s (to stand for the slope of the regression of log V on r), and dr/dt by the derivative of the right-hand side of equation (31):

$$\frac{1}{Y}\frac{dY}{dt} = s \cdot \frac{d}{dt}\left[\frac{1}{Y}\frac{dY}{dt}\right]^* + \frac{1}{M}\frac{dM}{dt}. \tag{38}$$

Assume that the anticipated rate of growth of income is determined by a simple adaptive expectations model:

$$\frac{d}{dt}\left[\frac{1}{Y}\frac{dY}{dt}\right]^* = \beta\left[\frac{1}{Y}\frac{dY}{dt} - \left(\frac{1}{Y}\frac{dY}{dt}\right)^*\right]. \tag{39}$$

Substitute equation (39) in equation (38) and solve for $(1/Y)(dY/dt)$. The result is

$$\frac{1}{Y}\frac{dY}{dt} = \left(\frac{1}{Y}\frac{dY}{dt}\right)^* + \frac{1}{1 - \beta s}\left[\frac{1}{M}\frac{dM}{dt} - \left(\frac{1}{Y}\frac{dY}{dt}\right)^*\right]. \tag{40}$$

Subtract $(1/M)(dM/dt)$ from both sides, and equation (40) can also be written

$$\frac{1}{V}\frac{dV}{dt} = \frac{\beta s}{1 - \beta s}\left[\frac{1}{M}\frac{dM}{dt} - \frac{1}{Y^*}\frac{dY^*}{dt}\right]. \qquad (41)$$

Assume that $0 < \beta s < 1$.[24] Equations (40) and (41) give a very simple and appealing result. If the rate of change of money equals the anticipated rate of change of nominal income, then nominal income changes at the same rate as money—we are in the simple quantity equation world. If the rate of change of money exceeds the anticipated rate of change of nominal income, so will the actual rate of change of nominal income, which will also exceed the rate of change of money—velocity is increasing in a "boom." Conversely for a "contraction" or "recession," interpreted as a slower rate of growth in the actual than in the anticipated rate of growth of income.

Note that this way of introducing a procyclical movement in velocity is an alternative or complement to the approach I suggested in an earlier article (Friedman 1959 and 1969). There the procyclical movement of velocity was explained by the difference between measured and permanent income. The two approaches are not mutually exclusive— as I indicated in my earlier article, when I left room for interest rate effects on velocity (Friedman 1969, pp. 130–136). In the present context, the simplest way to introduce both effects would be to rewrite (12b) as

$$M^D = Y^* l(r), \qquad (12c)$$

where Y^* is permanent nominal income. To complete the system, equation (14) must be replaced with a more sophisticated adjustment mechanism involving Y—otherwise the system, with Y^* treated as determined by the past history of Y, would be overdetermined. Such a more sophisticated mechanism is discussed in section 12 below.

In summary, the key elements of the monetary theory of nominal income are:

(a) A unit elasticity of the demand for money with respect to real income.

(b) A nominal market interest rate equal to the anticipated real rate plus the anticipated rate of change of prices, kept at that level by speculators with firmly held anticipations.

(c) A difference between the anticipated real interest rate and the real secular rate of growth determined outside the system.

[24] This is the condition for dynamic stability of the system. See Cagan 1956.

(d) Full and instantaneous adjustment of the amount of money demanded to the amount supplied.

These elements are borrowed mostly from Irving Fisher and John Maynard Keynes. Together they yield a simple two-equation system that determines the time path of nominal income but has nothing to say directly about the division of changes in nominal income between prices and quantity.

This simple model for analyzing short-term economic fluctuations seems to me more satisfactory than either the simple quantity theory which takes real output as determined outside the system and regards economic fluctuations as a mirror image of changes in the quantity of money or the simple Keynesian income-expenditure theory which takes prices as determined outside the system and regards economic fluctuations as a mirror image of changes in autonomous expenditures.

10. Comparison of the Three Approaches

None of the three simple theories—the simple quantity theory, the simple income-expenditure theory, the simple monetary theory of nominal income—professes to be a complete, fully worked out analysis of short-term fluctuations in aggregate economic magnitudes. All are to be interpreted rather as frameworks for such analyses, establishing the broad categories within which further elaborations will proceed.

The simple quantity theory puts in center stage the relation at each point in time between a particular flow—the flow of spending or income—and a particular stock—the quantity of money. The simple income-expenditure theory emphasizes the relation at each point in time between two components of the flow of income—autonomous and induced spending. The simple monetary theory of nominal income emphasizes the relation between the flow of income at each point in time and the past history of the quantity of money.

The simple quantity theory and the simple income-expenditure theory have six common elements, in addition to sharing the same six-equation model, that deserve emphasis because they indicate what are the main unresolved problems.

1. Both analyze short-run adjustments in terms of shifts from one static equilibrium position to another.

2. Both implicitly regard each equilibrium position as characterized by a stable *level* of prices or output. Neither explicitly introduces changing prices or changing output into the formal theoretical analysis.

The recent proliferation of formal growth models and the even more recent introduction of monetary change into them are attempts to fill this gap.[25]

3. Both regard interest rates as adjusting instantaneously to a new equilibrium level—in the quantity theory, to equate saving and investment; in the income-expenditure theory, to equate quantity of money demanded and supplied. This is a retrogression from Irving Fisher's earlier work.

4. Neither model gives any explicit role to anticipations about economic magnitudes. The income-expenditure theory comes closer to doing so in terms of the role that Keynes assigned to expectations about long-term interest rates, which could be incorporated in equation (12), as we did in equation (8). Here again, there has been much recent work directed at filling this gap.[26]

5. Both fill in the missing equation by an assumption that is not part of the basic theoretical analysis. This is less blatant, in one sense, for the quantity theory, since at least there is a well-developed economic theory, summarized in the Walrasian equations of general equilibrium, that explains what determines the level of output, so that the equations chosen for analysis can be regarded as a subset of a complete system. That is why, as agreement has been reached on the fallaciousness of Keynes's proposition (1), essentially all economic theorists, whatever model they prefer for short-run analysis, accept the quantity-theory model, completed by the Walrasian equations, as valid for long-run equilibrium.[27] The rigid price assumption of Keynes is, in this sense, much more arbitrary. It is entirely a *deus ex machina* with no underpinning in economic theory. Moreover, given that the price level in the long run is determined by the quantity-theory model, there is no theoretical link between the short-run model and the long-run model, no way of connecting the one to the other.

6. One aspect of the preceding point is so important that it deserves to be stated explicitly and separately. Neither theoretical model has anything to say about the factors that determine the proportions in which a change in nominal income will, in the short run, be divided between price change and output change. One theory *asserts* that the change in nominal income will all be absorbed by price change; the other, that it

[25] Some of the more important items are Solow (1956), Mundell (1965), Tobin (1965), Johnson (1967a, 1967b), Uzawa (1966), Sidrauski (1967a, 1967b), Levhari and Patinkin (1968), and Friedman (1969, chap. 1).
[26] Some of the more important items are Koyck (1954), Cagan (1956), Friedman (1957), Nerlove (1958), Muth (1960), Solow (1960), Allais (1966).
[27] See, for example, the model in Bailey (1962, pp. 33–36, 40–42).

will all be absorbed by quantity change. In my opinion, this is the central common defect of the two approaches as theories of short-run change.

The third approach differs significantly in regard to the elements that are common to the simple quantity theory and simple income-expenditure theory.

1. It does not, as they do, analyze short-run adjustments in terms of shifts from one static equilibrium position to another. It embodies a dynamic adjustment process.

2. It does not, as they do, regard each equilibrium position as characterized by a stable *level* of prices or output. It encompasses steady growth in prices or output as long-run equilibrium positions.

3. It does not regard interest rates as adjusting instantaneously to a new equilibrium level because it allows for a change in interest rates along with a change in the anticipated rate of change of prices. However, it does neglect the effect of other factors on interest rates (the saving-investment process stressed by the quantity theory; the effect of changes in the nominal quantity of money stressed by the income expenditure theory) except as they affect the course of nominal income and, in consequence, the anticipated rate of change of prices.

4. It does, unlike the other approaches, give an explicit role to anticipations about economic magnitudes. The differences between anticipated and actual magnitudes are the motive force behind the short-run fluctuations.

5. Like the others, it fills in the missing equation by an assumption that is not part of the basic theoretical analysis. The assumption (that speculators determine the interest rate in accord with firmly held anticipations, and that the difference between the permanent real interest rate and the secular growth of output can be taken as a constant for short period fluctuations) is intermediate between the others in its link to economic theory. It is not as clearly linked to a well-developed body of theory as the simple quantity approach is to the Walrasian equations of general equilibrium, yet it has more of a link to theory than does the rigid price assumption of Keynes. Further, like the quantity approach and unlike the income-expenditure approach, there is a theoretical link between the short-run model and the long-run model.

6. The chief defect that this model shares in common with the other two is that none of the three has anything to say about the factors that determine the proportions in which a change in nominal income will, in the short run, be divided between price change and output change— the topic with which section 12 below deals. The one advantage in this

respect of the third approach is that it does not make any assertion about this division as both the others do. It is, as it were, orthogonal to that issue and can therefore be more easily linked to alternative theories about that division.

11. Correspondence of the Monetary Theory of Nominal Income with Experience

I have not before this written down explicitly the particular simplification I have labelled the monetary theory of nominal income—though Meltzer has referred to the theory underlying our *Monetary History* as a "theory of nominal income" (Meltzer 1965, p. 414).[28] But once written down, it rings the bell, and seems to me to correspond to the broadest framework implicit in much of the work that I and others have done in analyzing monetary experience. It seems also to be consistent with many of our findings. I do not propose here to attempt a full catalogue, but wish to suggest a number, and, more important, to indicate the chief defect that I find in the framework.

One finding that we have observed is that the relation between changes in the nominal quantity of money and changes in nominal income is almost always closer and more dependable than the relation between changes in real income and the real quantity of money or between changes in the quantity of money per unit of output and changes in prices.[29] This result has always seemed to me puzzling, since a stable demand function for money with an income elasticity different from unity led us to expect the opposite. Yet the actual finding would be generated by the monetary approach outlined in this paper, with the division between prices and quantities determined by variables not explicitly contained in it.

Another broad finding is the procyclical pattern of velocity, which can be rationalized either by the distinction between permanent and measured income or, as in the monetary approach, by the effect of changes in the anticipated rate of change in prices.

[28] However, he referred to it as a "long-run theory of nominal income," whereas the theory outlined in section 8 above is intended to be a short-run theory. We accept much of what Meltzer says about the theory underlying our *Monetary History,* but also disagree with much of it; in particular, the way he introduces real income and changes in real income into the analysis. This is strictly *ad hoc* and renders the asserted theory a logically open and underdetermined theory.

[29] However, Walters reports a different result for Britain for the period since the end of World War I—a closer relation with prices in the interwar period and with real output in the post-World War II period (Walters, 1970, p. 52).

On still another level, the approach is consistent with much of the work that Fisher did on interest rates, and also the more recent work by Anna Schwartz and myself, Gibson, Kaufman, Cagan, and others. In particular, the approach provides an interpretation of the empirical generalization that high interest rates mean that money has been easy, in the sense of increasing rapidly, and low interest rates, that money has been tight, in the sense of increasing slowly, rather than the reverse.

Again, the approach is consistent with the importance we have been led to attach to *rates of change* in money rather than levels, and, in particular, to changes in the rate of change in explaining short-term fluctuations.

The approach is consistent also with the success of the equations constructed by Andersen and Jordan at St. Louis relating changes in nominal income to current and past changes in the quantity of money (Andersen and Jordan 1968).

The chief defect of the approach is that it does not give a satisfactory explanation of the lags in the reaction of velocity and interest rates at turning points in monetary rates of change.[30] These lags are significant for cyclical analysis. They are less relevant for a study of monetary trends. Because of this defect, the movements of velocity and interest rates in the first nine months or so after a distinct change in the rate of

[30] We know, for example, that when the rate of growth of the quantity of money declines, the rate of change of income will not show any appreciable effect for something like six to nine months (for the United States) on the average. During this interval, interest rates typically continue to rise, indeed generally at an accelerated pace. After the interval, both velocity and interest rates start to decline.

This result is not necessarily inconsistent with the monetary approach outlined here. Suppose that prior to the decline in the rate of monetary growth the system was not in full equilibrium, so that the actual rate of growth of nominal income $(1/Y)(dY/dt)$ was higher than the anticipated rate of growth $[(1/Y)(dY/dt)]^*$. Then, even the new rate of monetary growth could be higher than the anticipated rate, implying from equation (41) a further rise in velocity, from equation (40), a larger actual than anticipated rise in nominal income, from equation (39), a further rise in the anticipated rate, and from equation (31), a further rise in the nominal interest rate. These would continue until the anticipated rate had risen to equality with the new rate of monetary growth.

However, this reaction would imply a slower rate of rise in velocity and interest rates than prior to the monetary turning point, whereas our impression is that the opposite often occurs. More important, even if the system is not in full equilibrium prior to a decline in the rate of monetary growth, the decline in monetary growth, if large enough, will make the new rate of monetary growth less than $[(1/Y)(dY/dt)]^*$. In that case, equations (41), (40), (39), and (31) would produce a decline in velocity and in interest rates contemporaneous with the decline in the rate of monetary growth. Yet the lag in reaction is highly consistent and, in particular, seems to be independent of the size of the change in the rate of monetary growth.

monetary growth cannot be satisfactorily explained by the monetary theory of nominal income. If these periods were cut out of the historical record, my impression is that the model would fit the rest of the record very well—not of course without error but with errors that are on the modest side as aggregate economic hypotheses go.

Periods just after turning points can, I believe, be explained best by incorporating two elements so far omitted. The first is a revision of equation (14) to allow for a difference between actual and desired money balances, as in equation (48), below. The second is a weakening of equation (25) to permit a stronger liquidity effect on interest rates.

12. The Adjustment Process

The key need to remedy the defects common to all the models I have sketched is a theory that will explain (a) the short-run division of a change in nominal income between prices and output, (b) the short-run adjustment of nominal income to a change in autonomous variables, and (c) the transition between this short-run situation and a long-run equilibrium.[31]

In the rest of this paper, the central idea I shall use in sketching the direction in which such a theory might be developed is the distinction between actual and anticipated magnitudes or, to use a terminology that need not be identical but that I shall treat for this purpose as if it is, between measured and permanent magnitudes. At a long-run equilibrium position, all anticipations are realized, so that actual and anticipated magnitudes, or measured and permanent magnitudes, are equal.[32]

I shall regard long-run equilibrium as determined by the earlier quantity-theory model plus the Walrasian equations of general equilibrium. In a full statement, the earlier model should be expanded by including wealth in the consumption and liquidity-preference functions,

[31] Still other parts of the theoretical framework are developed more fully in the course of the empirical analysis of some of the issues raised in the other chapters of the book from which this paper is abstracted.

[32] Note that the equality of actual and anticipated magnitudes is a necessary but not a sufficient condition for a long-run equilibrium position. In principle, actual and anticipated magnitudes could be equal along an adjustment path between one equilibrium position and another. The corresponding proposition is more complicated for measured and permanent magnitudes and depends on the precise definition of these terms. However, since we shall be considering a special case in which the stated condition is treated as both necessary and sufficient for long-run equilibrium, these complications can be bypassed.

and the capital stock in the investment function, and by allowing for steady growth in output and prices.

I shall regard short-run equilibrium as determined by an adjustment process in which the rate of adjustment in a variable is a function of the discrepancy between the measured and the anticipated value of that variable or its rate of change, as well as, perhaps, of other variables or their rates of change. Finally, I shall let at least some anticipated variables be determined by a feedback process from past observed values.

a) Division of a Change in Nominal Income between Prices and Output

It seems plausible that the division of a change in nominal income between prices and output depends on two major factors: anticipations about the behavior of prices—this is the inertia factor stressed by Keynes—and the current level of output or employment compared with the full-employment (permanent) level of output or employment—this is the supply-demand response stressed by quantity theorists. We can express this in general form as:

$$\frac{dP}{dt} = f\left[\frac{dY}{dt}, \left(\frac{dP}{dt}\right)^*, \left(\frac{dy}{dt}\right)^*, y, y^*\right], \tag{42}$$

$$\frac{dy}{dt} = g\left[\frac{dY}{dt}, \left(\frac{dP}{dt}\right)^*, \left(\frac{dy}{dt}\right)^*, y, y^*\right], \tag{43}$$

where an asterisk attached to a variable denotes the anticipated value of that variable and where the form of equations (42) and (43) must be consistent with the identity

$$Y = Py, \tag{44}$$

so that only one of equations (42) and (43) is independent.

To illustrate, a specific linearized version of equations (42) and (43) might be

$$\frac{d \log P}{dt} = \left(\frac{d \log P}{dt}\right)^* + \alpha\left[\frac{d \log Y}{dt} - \left(\frac{d \log Y}{dt}\right)^*\right] + \gamma[\log y - (\log y)^*]; \tag{45}$$

$$\frac{d \log y}{dt} = \left(\frac{d \log y}{dt}\right)^* + (1 - \alpha)\left[\frac{d \log Y}{dt} - \left(\frac{d \log Y}{dt}\right)^*\right] - \gamma[\log y - (\log y)^*]. \tag{46}$$

The sum of these is exactly the logarithm of equation (44), differentiated with respect to time, provided the anticipated variables also satisfy a corresponding identity,[33] so the equations satisfy the specified conditions.

The simple quantity theory assumption, that all of the change in income is in prices, and that output is always at its permanent level, is obtained by setting $\alpha = 1$ and $\gamma = \infty$. An infinite value of γ corresponds to "perfectly flexible prices" and assures that $y = y^*$. The unit value of α assures that prices absorb any change in nominal income, so that real income grows at its long-term rate of growth.[34]

The simple Keynesian assumption, that all of the change in income is in output, so long as there is unemployment, and all in prices, once there is full employment, is obtained by setting $[(d \log P)/(dt)]^* = 0$, and $\alpha = \gamma = 0$ for $y < y^*$, and then shifting to the quantity theory specification of $\alpha = 1$, $\gamma = \infty$ for $y \geq y^*$. The zero value of $[(d \log P)/dt]^*$ assures that anticipations are for stable prices and, combined with the zero values of α and γ, that $(d \log P)/(dt) = 0$. It would be somewhat more general, and perhaps more consistent with the spirit rather than the letter of Keynes's analysis, and even more that of his modern followers, to let $[(d \log P)/(dt)]^*$ differ from zero while keeping $\alpha = \gamma = 0$ for $y < y^*$. This would introduce the kind of price rigidity relevant to Keynes's short-period analysis, yet could be regarded as capturing the phenomenon that his modern followers have emphasized as cost-push inflation.

The simple monetary theory of nominal income is of course consistent with these equations in their general form since it does not specify anything about the division of a change in nominal income between prices and output.

In their general form, equations (45) and (46) do not by themselves specify the path of prices or output beginning with any initial position. In addition, we need to know how anticipated values are formed. Presumably these are affected by the course of events so that, in response to a disturbance which produces a discrepancy between actual and anticipated values of the variables, there is a feedback effect that brings the actual and anticipated variables together again (see

---

[33] This also explains why $[(d \log y)/(dt)]^*$ does not appear explicitly in equation (45), or $[(d \log P)/(dt)]^*$ in equation (46), as they do in equations (42) and (43). They are implicitly included in $[(d \log Y)/(dt)]^*$.

[34] With γ infinity, and $\log y = \log y^*$, the final expression in equations (45) and (46) is $\infty \cdot 0$, or technically indeterminate. The product can be taken to be zero in general, except possibly for a few isolated points at which $\log y$ deviates from $\log y^*$, a deviation closed instantaneously by infinite rates of change in $\log P$ and $\log y$.

below). If this process proceeds rapidly, then the transitory adjustments defined by equations (45) and (46) are of little significance. The relevant analysis is the analysis which connects the asterisked variables.

b) Short-Run Adjustment of Nominal Income

For monetary theory, the key question is the process of adjustment to a discrepancy between the nominal quantity of money demanded and the nominal quantity supplied. Such a discrepancy could arise from either a change in the supply of money (a shift in the supply function) or a change in the demand for money (a shift in the demand function). The key insight of the quantity-theory approach is that such a discrepancy will be manifested primarily in attempted spending, thence in the rate of change in nominal income. Put differently, money holders cannot determine the nominal quantity of money (though their reactions may introduce feedback effects that will affect the nominal quantity of money), but they can make velocity anything they wish.

What, on this view, will cause the rate of change in nominal income to depart from its permanent value? Anything that produces a discrepancy between the nominal quantity of money demanded and the quantity supplied, or between the two rates of change of money demanded and money supplied. In general form

$$\frac{dY}{dt} = f\left[\left(\frac{dY}{dt}\right)^*, \frac{dM^S}{dt}, \frac{dM^D}{dt}, M^S, M^D\right], \tag{47}$$

where M^S refers to money supplied, M^D refers to money demanded, and the two symbols are used to indicate that the two are not necessarily equal. That is, equation (47) replaces the adjustment equation (14), $M^D = M^S$, common to all the simple models, as well as the special adjustment equation (41) derived from the monetary theory of nominal income.

To illustrate, a particular linearized version of equation (47) would be

$$\frac{d \log Y}{dt} = \left(\frac{d \log Y}{dt}\right)^* + \Psi\left(\frac{d \log M^S}{dt} - \frac{d \log M^D}{dt}\right) + \Phi\left(\log M^S - \log M^D\right). \tag{48}$$

Unlike equations (45) and (46), the two final adjustment terms on the right-hand side do not explicitly include any asterisked magnitudes. But implicitly they do. The amount of money demanded will depend on anticipated permanent income and prices as well as on the anticipated rate of change in prices.

The three simple models considered earlier all require setting $\Phi = \infty$ in equation (48) to assure that $M^s = M^D$. However, once this is done, the rest of the equation provides no information on the adjustment process, since the final term, which is of the form $\infty \cdot 0$ is indeterminate. Hence, even though $M^s = M^D$ implies that

$$\frac{d \log M^s}{dt} = \frac{d \log M^D}{dt}, \tag{49}$$

so that the second term on the right-hand side of equation (48) is zero for any finite value of Ψ, it does not follow that

$$\frac{d \log Y}{dt} = \left(\frac{d \log Y}{dt}\right)^*. \tag{50}$$

The requirement (49) leads to the equation

$$\frac{d \log Y}{dt} = \frac{d \log M}{dt} \tag{51}$$

for the simple quantity theory since, with real income and the interest rate fixed, the quantity of money demanded is proportional to prices and hence to nominal income. This equation says that a change in money supply is reflected immediately and proportionately in nominal income.

For the simple Keynesian theory, equation (49) leads, from equation (22), to

$$\frac{d \log M}{dt} = \left[\frac{\partial \log l}{d \log Y} + \frac{\partial \log l}{\partial r} \frac{dr}{d \log Y}\right] \frac{d \log Y}{dt} \tag{52}$$

where $dr/d \log Y$ is to be calculated from equation (21), the IS curve. In the special case of absolute liquidity preference $\partial \log l/\partial r = \infty$; in the special case of completely inelastic investment and saving functions, $dr/d \log Y = \infty$. In either of these cases, equation (52) implies that, for $d \log M/dt$ finite, $d \log Y/dt = 0$; i.e., a change in the supply of money has no influence on income. In the more general case, equation (52) says that a change in money supply is reflected immediately, but not necessarily proportionately, in nominal income.

For the monetary theory of nominal income, equation (49) implies, as we have seen earlier, equation (41), which allows for a delayed adjustment of permanent income to measured income, but not for any discrepancy between M^s and M^D.

In its general form, equation (48) allows for changes in both supply of money and demand for money. It also implicitly allows for the forces emphasized by Keynes, shifts in investment or other autonomous expenditures, through the effect of such changes on M^S and M^D. For example, an autonomous rise in investment demand will tend to raise interest rates. The rise in interest rates will tend to reduce M^D, introducing a discrepancy in one or both of the bracketed expressions on the right-hand side of equation (48), which will cause $(d \log Y)/(dt)$ to exceed $[(d \log Y)/(dt)]^*$.

c) Money Demand and Supply Functions

As this comment indicates, in order to complete the theory of the adjustment process, it is necessary to specify the functions connecting M^D and M^S with other variables in the system, and also to provide relations determining any additional variables—such as interest rates—entering into these functions. Sections 3 and 4 above discuss the demand and supply functions for money that we regard as relevant for this purpose, so only a few brief supplementary comments are required for present purposes.

First, in much of our empirical work we have taken M^S itself as an autonomous variable and have not incorporated in the analysis any feedback from other adjustments. A major reason that we have done so is our judgment that the supply function has varied greatly from time to time.

Second, in the notation we have been using in this section, the variables y and $(1/P)(dP/dt)$ in equation (7) should have asterisks attached to them.

Third, the function specifying M^D might in principle include a transitory component. That is, there is nothing inconsistent with the theory here sketched and distinguishing between a short-run and long-run demand for money, as some writers have done (Heller 1965; Chow 1966; Konig 1968).

d) Determination of Interest Rates

Given that interest rates enter into the demand function for money (equation [7]) and also, presumably, into the supply function, a complete model must specify the factors determining them. Our long-run model determines their permanent values. So what is needed is an analysis of the adjustment process for interest rates comparable with that for prices and nominal income discussed above—provided, as seems reasonable, that measured as well as permanent values of interest rates enter into the money demand and supply functions.

The monetary theory of nominal income incorporates one possible adjustment process—via the anticipated rate of price change. We have not worked out the formal theory of a more sophisticated adjustment process in any detail. The one aspect we have considered is the effect of changes in M^s on interest rates.[35] In that analysis, we have in effect regarded interest rates as adjusting very rapidly to clear the market for loanable funds, the supply of loanable funds as being possibly linked to changes in M^s, and the demand for and supply of loanable funds expressed as a function of the nominal interest rate as depending on Y and $[(1/P)\ (dP/dt)]^*$ along with other variables.

In some of our empirical work, we have treated interest rates as exogenous.

e) Determination of Anticipated Values

The transition between the short-run adjustment process and long-run equilibrium is produced by an adjustment of anticipated values to measured values in such a way that, for a stable system, a single disturbance will set up discrepancies that will in the course of time be eliminated. To put this in general terms, we must have

$$\left[\frac{d \log P}{dt}\ (t)\right]^* = f\left[\frac{d \log P}{dT}\ (T)\right], \tag{53}$$

$$\left[\frac{d \log Y}{dt}\ (t)\right]^* = g\left[\frac{d \log Y}{dT}\ (T)\right], \tag{54}$$

$$y^*(t) = h[y(T)], \tag{55}$$

$$P^*(t) = j[P(T)], \tag{56}$$

where t stands for a particular point in time and T for a vector of all dates prior to t.

A disturbance of long-term equilibrium, let us say, introduces discrepancies in the two final terms in parentheses on the right-hand side of equation (48). This will cause the rate of change in nominal income to deviate from its permanent value, which through equations (45) and (46) produces deviations in the rate of price change and output change from their permanent values. These may in turn re-enter equation (48) but whether they do or not, they will, through equations (53)–(56), produce changes in the anticipated values that will, sooner or later and perhaps after a cyclical reaction process, eliminate the discrepancies between measured and permanent values.

[35] See chapter 7 in the forthcoming book from which this paper is abstracted.

These anticipation equations are in one sense very general, in another, very special. They require that anticipations be determined entirely by the past history of the particular variable in question, not by other past history or other currently observed phenomena. These equations deny any "autonomous" role to anticipations. These equations, or preferable alternatives to them, are not directly related to the monetary issues that are the main concern of this paper, which is why I have treated them so summarily. Their only function here is to close the system.

One subtle problem in this kind of a structure, in which we have identified the absence of a discrepancy between actual and anticipated values as defining long-period equilibrium, is to assure that the feedback relations defined by equations (53)–(56), as well as the other functions, are consistent with the expanded system of Walrasian equations which specify the long-term equilibrium values. At least some values are implicitly determined in two ways: by a feedback relation such as equations (53) and (56), and by the system of long-run equilibrium equations. The problem is to assure that at long-run equilibrium these two determinations do not conflict.

In our empirical work, we have generally used a particular form of anticipated function, namely, one which defines the anticipated values as a declining weighted average of past observed values. For example, a specific form of equation (55) is

$$y^*(t) = \beta \int_{T=-\infty}^{t} e^{(\beta-\alpha)(t-T)} y(T) dT, \tag{57}$$

where α and β are parameters, α defining the long-term rate of growth, and β, the speed of adjustment of anticipations to experiences (Friedman 1957, pp. 142–47).

13. An Illustration

It may help to clarify the general nature of this theoretical approach if we apply it to a hypothetical monetary disturbance.

Let us start with a situation of full equilibrium with stable prices and full employment and with output growing at, say, 3 percent per year. For simplicity, assume that the income elasticity of demand for money is unity, so that the quantity of money is also growing at the rate of 3 percent per year. Assume also that money is wholly non-interest-bearing fiat money and that its quantity can be taken as autonomous.

Assume that there is a shift at time $t = t_0$ in the rate of growth of the quantity of money from 3 percent per year to, say, 8 percent per year and that this new rate of growth is maintained indefinitely. Figure 1 shows the time path of the money stock before and after time t_0. These figures are not drawn strictly to scale. For emphasis, they exaggerate the difference in the slopes of the lines before and after t_0.

a) Long-Run Equilibrium

Let us first ask what the long-run equilibrium solution will be. Clearly, after full adjustment, nominal income will be rising at 8 percent per year. If, for the moment, we neglect any effect of this monetary change on real output and the rate of growth of output, this means that prices would be rising at 5 percent per year. It might therefore seem as if the equilibrium path of nominal income would duplicate that of the quantity of money in figure 1 (redrawn as the solid plus dashed line in fig. 2). But this is not the case. With prices rising at the rate of 5 percent per year and, at equilibrium, with this price rise fully anticipated by everyone, it is now more costly to hold money. As a result, equation (7)

FIGURE 1

Time Path of Money Stock Before and After Time t_0

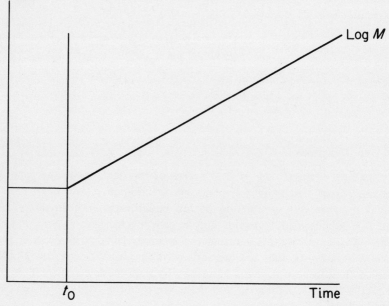

would indicate a decline in the real quantity of money demanded relative to income, that is, a rise in desired velocity. This rise would be achieved by a rise in nominal income over and above that required to match the rise in the nominal quantity of money. The equilibrium path of nominal income would be like the solid line in figure 2 rather than the dashed line.

If equilibrium real output and the rate of growth of real output were unaffected by the monetary change, as I have so far assumed, the equilibrium path of prices would be the same as that of nominal income, except that it would have a slope of 3 percent per year less, to allow for the growth in real income. However, equilibrium real output will not be unaffected by this monetary change. The exact effect depends on just how real output is measured, in particular whether it includes or excludes the nonpecuniary services of money. If it includes them, as in principle it should, then the level of real output will be lower after the monetary change than before. It will be lower for two reasons: first, the higher cost of holding cash balances will lead producers to substitute other resources for cash, which will lower productive efficiency; second,

FIGURE 2

Equilibrium Path of Nominal Income Before and After Time t_0

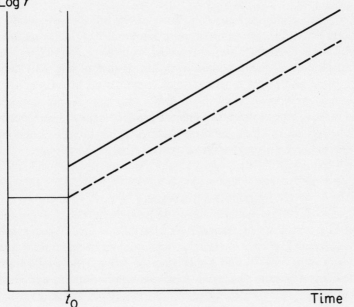

the flow of nonpecuniary services from money will be reduced (Friedman 1969, pp. 14–15). For both reasons, the price level of output will have to rise more than nominal income—a solid line and a dashed line like those for nominal income in figure 2 would be farther apart vertically for prices of final products than for nominal income.

It is harder to be precise about the equilibrium rate of growth, since that depends on the particular growth model. What is clear is that the aggregate stock of nonhuman capital, including money, will be lower relative to human capital, but that the aggregate stock of physical (non-money) capital will be higher, so that the real yield on capital (essentially our r_e of equation [7]) will be lower. The nominal interest rate (the r_b of equation [7]) will equal this real yield plus the rate of change in prices, so it will be higher. If these changes have any effect on the rate of growth of real output, they will tend to reduce it, so that the equilibrium price level of final products will not only be higher relative to its initial value than the equilibrium level of nominal income; it may also rise more rapidly (Stein 1966; Johnson 1967a, 1967b; Marty 1968). For simplicity, I shall neglect this possibility and assume that the equilibrium rate of rise in prices is 5 percent per year.

b) The Adjustment Process

So much for the equilibrium position. What of the adjustment process?

This description of the equilibrium position already tells us one thing about the adjustment process. In order to produce the shift in the equilibrium path of nominal income from the dashed to the solid line, nominal income and prices must rise over some period at a faster rate than the final equilibrium rate—at a faster rate than 8 percent per year for nominal income and 5 percent per year for prices. There must, that is, be a cyclical reaction, an overshooting, in the rate of change in nominal income and prices, though not necessarily in their levels.

How will this adjustment process be reflected in my theoretical sketch of the adjustment process? The shift in $(d \log M^s)/(dt)$ at time t_0 from 3 percent to 8 percent introduces a discrepancy of positive sign into the second term in parentheses of equation (48), while initially leaving the third term in parentheses unchanged. As a result, $(d \log Y)/(dt)$ will increase, exceeding $[(d \log Y)/(dt)]^*$, which, viewed in this transitional process as an anticipated value rather than as a long-run equilibrium value, is unchanged from the prior long-run equilibrium value. How rapidly the rate of growth of nominal income rises depends partly on the value of Ψ, the coefficient indicating speed of adjustment, and partly on the demand function for money. If the latter depends only on anticipated values (that is, if all the variables in equation [7] have asterisks), $(d \log M^D)/(dt)$ will initially be unchanged, so everything will depend on Ψ, which might have any value, from zero, meaning no adjustment, to a value higher than unity, meaning that nominal income would rise initially by more than 5 percent per year.[36]

Whatever the rate of rise in nominal income, it will be divided into a rise in prices and in output, in accordance with equations (45) and (46). If α is less than unity, both real output and prices will start rising, their relative rates depending on the size of α.

The rising prices and nominal income will start affecting anticipated rates of change, through equations (53) and (56), feeding back into (48) and (45) and (46).

All of this is so at time t_0, with no effect on the levels of any of the variables. However, as the process continues, the levels start being affected. In equation (48), $\log M^S$ comes to exceed $\log M^D$, so the second term of equation (48) adds to the upward pressure on $(d \log Y)/(dt)$, making for a speeding up in the expansion of nominal income. In equations (45) and (46), $\log y$ comes to exceed $\log y^*$, thus increasing the fraction of income increase absorbed by prices and reducing the fraction absorbed by output. The changed levels of y and P feed into equations (55) and (56) and so start altering y^* and P^*.

The changes in all of the variables now start affecting the demand functions for money, both directly, as these variables enter the demand functions, and indirectly, as they affect other variab'es, such as interest rates, which in turn enter the demand functions. As a result, $(d \log M^D)/(dt)$ and M^D in equation (48) start to change. The process will, of course, finally be completed when the relevant measured variables are all equal to their permanent counterparts and these equal the long-run equilibrium values discussed above.

It is impossible to carry much farther this verbal statement of the solution of an incompletely specified system of simultaneous differential equations. The precise adjustment path depends on how the missing elements of the system are specified and on the numerical values of the parameters, but perhaps this much is enough to give the flavor of the kind of adjustment process they generate, and to indicate why this process is necessarily cyclical.

What is the reflection in these equations of the point made in the second paragraph of this section, namely, that $(d \log Y)/(dt)$ and $(d$

---

[36] The model briefly sketched in the final two paragraphs of Friedman (1959) implicitly has an initial value of Ψ which is much higher than unity.

log $P)/(dt)$ must, during the transition, average higher than their final long-term equilibrium values? Consider equation (48). Suppose that over a period the *average* value of $(d \log Y)/(dt)$ and $(d \log P)/(dt)$ had been 8 percent per year and 5 percent per year, respectively. Suppose the anticipations functions (53) and (56) were such that this was fully reflected in anticipated values. Then, as we have seen, although M^S would have risen at the rate of 5 percent per year, M^D would not have; so the final term in equation (48) would not be zero, even though the middle term on the right-hand side might be. Hence, $(d \log Y)/(dt)$ would exceed $[(d \log Y)/(dt)]^*$, which by assumption is at its long-run equilibrium value; so full equilibrium would not have been attained.

Figure 3 summarizes various possible adjustment paths of $(d \log Y)/(dt)$ consistent with the theory sketched. The one common feature of all of them is that the area above the 8 percent line must exceed the

FIGURE 3

Possible Adjustment Paths of Rate of Change in Nominal Income

$$\frac{d \log Y}{dt}$$

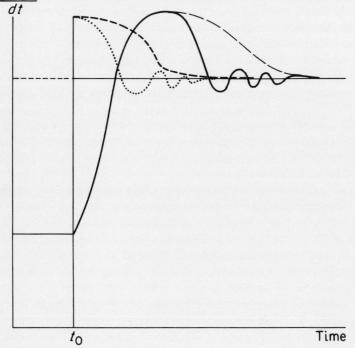

t_0 Time

area below. In principle, of course, still other paths are possible. For example, it is conceptually possible for the adjustment to be explosive rather than damped. Restricting ourselves to damped paths is an empirical judgment.

14. Conclusion

In concluding this discussion of a theoretical framework, it may be worth stating that it is not a framework special to me or to those economists who view the operation of the economy in terms of the quantity theory either in its simple form or in the form of the monetary theory of nominal income. No doubt other economists would expand the framework differently, stress different parts of it, elaborate points I have skimmed over, and skim over points I have elaborated. But almost all economists would accept the framework, and this is true even, I believe, of the least thorough part, the sketch of the adjustment process in the preceding two sections.

One purpose of setting forth this framework is to document my belief that the basic differences among economists are empirical, not theoretical: How important are changes in the supply of money compared with changes in the demand for money? Are transactions variables or asset variables most important in determining the demand for money? How elastic is the demand for money with respect to interest rates? With respect to the rate of change in prices? When changes in demand or supply occur that produce discrepancies between the quantity of money that the public holds and the quantity it desires to hold, how rapidly do these discrepancies tend to be eliminated? Does the adjustment impinge mostly on prices or mostly on quantities? Is the adjustment process cyclical or asymptotic? Is the adjustment to sharp changes over short periods different in kind or only in degree from the adjustment to slower changes over longer periods? How long does it take for people to alter their anticipations in light of experience?

Much of the controversy that has swirled about the role of money in economic affairs reflects, in my opinion, different implicit or explicit answers to these empirical questions. The reason such differences have been able to persist is, I believe, that full adjustment to monetary disturbances takes a very long time and affects many economic magnitudes. If adjustment were swift, immediate, and mechanical, as some earlier quantity theorists may have believed, or, more likely, as was attributed to them by their critics, the role of money would be clearly and sharply etched even in the imperfect figures that have been available. But, if the adjustment is slow, delayed, and sophisticated, then crude evidence may be misleading, and a more subtle examination of the record may be needed to disentangle what is systematic from what is random and erratic. That, not the elaboration of the theory, is the primary aim of the monograph from which this paper is adapted, as well as of the other monetary studies of the National Bureau.

References

Allais, M. "A Restatement of the Quantity Theory of Money." *A.E.R.* (December 1966), pp. 1123–57.

Andersen, Leonall C., and Jordan, Jerry L. "Monetary and Fiscal Actions: A Test of their Relative Importance in Economic Stabilization." *Review,* Federal Reserve Bank of St. Louis (November 1968), pp. 11–23.

Bailey, Martin J. *National Income and the Price Level.* New York: McGraw-Hill, 1962.

Baumol, W. J. "The Transactions Demand for Cash: An Inventory Theoretic Approach." *Q.J.E.* (November 1952), pp. 545–56.

Brainard, William. "Financial Institutions and a Theory of Monetary Control." In *Financial Markets and Economic Activity.* Cowles Foundation Monograph 21. New York: Wiley, 1967.

Brunner, Karl. "The 'Monetarist Revolution' in Monetary Theory." *Weltwirtschaftliches Archiv* 105, No. 1 (1970), pp. 1–30.

Brunner, Karl, and Meltzer, Allan H. "Predicting Velocity." *J. Finance* (May 1963), pp. 319–34.

Cagan, Phillip. "The Monetary Dynamics of Hyperinflation." In *Studies in the Quantity Theory of Money,* edited by Milton Friedman. Chicago: Univ. Chicago Press, 1956.

———. *Determinants and Effects of Changes in the Stock of Money, 1875–1960.* New York: Columbia Univ. Press (for Nat. Bur. Econ. Res.), 1965.

Chow, Gregory C. "On the Long-Run and Short-Run Demand for Money." *J.P.E.* 74 (April 1966):111–31.

Culbertson, J. M. "United States Monetary History: Its Implications for Monetary Theory." *Nat. Banking Rev.* (March 1964), pp. 372–75.

Fisher, Irving. *The Purchasing Power of Money.* New York: Macmillan, 1911.

———. "Money, Prices, Credit, and Banking." *A.E.R.* (June 1919), pp. 407–9.

Friedman, Milton. "The Quantity Theory of Money—a Restatement." In *Studies in the Quantity Theory of Money,* edited by M. Friedman. Chicago: Univ. Chicago Press, 1956. Reprinted in Friedman (1969).

———. *A Theory of the Consumption Function.* Princeton, N.J.: Princeton Univ. Press (for Nat. Bur. Econ. Res.), 1957.

———. "The Supply of Money and Changes in Prices and Output." In *The Relationship of Prices to Economic Stability and Growth,* pp. 241–56. U.S. Congress, Joint Economic Committee, Compendium, 1958. Reprinted in Friedman (1969).

————. "The Demand for Money: Some Theoretical and Empirical Results." *J.P.E.* 67 (August 1959):327–51. Reprinted as Occasional Paper 68 (New York: Nat. Bur. Econ. Res., 1959) and in Friedman (1969).

————. "The Lag in Effect of Monetary Policy." *J.P.E.* 69 (October 1961), pp. 447–66. Reprinted in Friedman (1969).

————. *Price Theory.* Chicago: Aldine, 1962.

————. "Interest Rates and the Demand for Money." *J. Law and Econ.* (October 1966), pp 71–85. Reprinted in Friedman (1969).

————. "The Monetary Theory and Policy of Henry Simons." *J. Law and Econ.* (October 1967), pp. 1–13. Reprinted in Friedman (1969).

————. "Money, Quantity Theory." In *International Encyclopedia of the Social Sciences*, pp. 432–47. New York: Macmillan and Free Press, 1968. (*a*)

————. "The Role of Monetary Policy." *A.E.R.* (March 1968), pp. 1–17. (*b*) Reprinted in Friedman (1969).

————. *The Optimum Quantity of Money and Other Essays.* Chicago: Aldine, 1969.

————. "A Theoretical Framework for Monetary Analysis," *J.P.E.* 78 (March-April 1970):193–238. (a)

————. "The Counter-Revolution in Monetary Theory." *Occasional Paper 33* (The Institute of Economic Affairs for Wincott Foundation). London: Tonbridge, 1970 (b).

————. "A Monetary Theory of Nominal Income." *J.P.E.* 79 (March-April 1971).

Friedman, Milton, and Meiselman, David. "The Relative Stability of the Investment Multipler and Monetary Velocity in the United Sttates, 1897–1958." *Stabilization Policies.* Englewood Cliffs, N.J.: Prentice-Hall, 1963.

Friedman, Milton, and Schwartz, Anna. "Money and Business Cycles." *Rev. Econ. and Statis.*, supp. (February 1963), pp. 32–64. Reprinted in Friedman (1969). (*a*).

————. *A Monetary History of the United States, 1867–1960.* Princeton, N.J.: Princeton Univ. Press, (for Nat. Bur. Econ. Res.), 1963. (*b*)

————. *Monetary Statistics of the United States.* New York: Columbia Univ. Press (for Nat. Bur. Econ. Res.), 1970.

Goldfeld, Stephen M. *Commercial Bank Behavior and Economic Activity.* Amsterdam: North-Holland, 1966.

Gramley, Lyle, and Chase, S. B., Jr. "Time Deposits in Monetary Analysis," *Federal Reserve Bull.* 51 (October 1965):1380–1406.

Gupta, Suraj. "Expected Rate of Change of Prices and Rates of Interest." Ph.D. dissertation, University of Chicago, 1964.

Haberler, Gottfried. *Prosperity and Depression.* 3d ed. Geneva: League of Nations, 1941.

Heller, H. R. "The Demand for Money: The Evidence from the Short-Run Data." *Q.J.E.* (May 1965), pp. 291–303.

Hendershott, Patric H. *The Neutralized Money Stock.* Homewood, Ill.: Irwin, 1968.

Hester, Donald, and Tobin, James, eds. *Financial Markets and Economic Activity.* Cowles Foundation Monograph 21. New York: Wiley, 1967.

Hicks, J. R. "Mr. Keynes and the Classics: A Suggested Interpretation." *Econometrica* 5 (April 1937):147–59. Reprinted in *Readings in the Theory of Income Distribution*, edited by W. Fellner and B. F. Haley. Homewood, Ill.: Irwin, 1951.

Holzman, Franklyn D., and Bronfenbrenner, Martin. "Survey of Inflation Theory." *A.E.R.* (September 1963), pp. 593–661.

Johnson, Harry G. "The *General Theory* after Twenty-Five Years." *A.E.R.* (May 1961), pp. 1–17.

————. "The Neo-classical One-Sector Growth Model: A Geometrical Exposition and Extension to a Monetary Economy." In *Essays in Monetary Economics*. London: Allen & Unwin, 1967. (*a*)

————. "Neutrality of Money in Growth Models: A Reply." *Economica* (February 1967), pp. 73–74. (*b*)

Keynes, John M. *The General Theory of Employment, Interest and Money*. London: Macmillan, 1936.

Konig, H. "Demand Function, Short-Run and Long-Run Function, and the Distributed Lag." *Zeitschrift Gesamte Staatswissenschaft* (February 1968), pp. 124 ff.

Koyck, L. M. *Distributed Lags and Investment Analysis*. Amsterdam: North-Holland, 1954.

Laurent, Robert. "Currency Transfers by Denominations." Ph.D. dissertation, Univ. Chicago, 1969.

Leijonhufvud, Axel. *On Keynesian Economics and the Economics of Keynes*. London: Oxford Univ. Press, 1968.

Levhari, D., and Patinkin, D. "The Role of Money in a Simple Growth Model." *A.E.R.* (September 1968), pp. 713–53.

Martin, P. W. *The Flaw in the Price System*. London: King, 1924.

Marty, Alvin. "The Optimal Rate of Growth of Money." *J.P.E.* 76, pt. 2 (July-August 1968):860–73.

Meltzer, Allan H. "The Demand for Money: The Evidence from the Time Series." *J.P.E.* 71 (June 1963):219–46.

————. "Monetary Theory and Monetary History." *Schweizerische Zeitschrift Volkswirtschaft und Statistik*, no. 4 (1965), pp. 409–22.

Mitchell, W. C. *Business Cycles*. New York: Nat. Bur. Econ. Res., 1927.

Mundell, Robert A. "A Fallacy in the Interpretation of Macro-economic Equilibrium." *J.P.E.* 73 (February 1965):61–66.

Muth, J. F. "Optimal Properties of Exponentally Weighted Forecasts." *J. American Statis. Assoc.* (June 1960), pp. 299–306.

Nerlove, Marc. *Distributed Lags and Demand Analysis*. Agriculture Handbook no. 141. Washington: Dept. Agriculture, 1958.

Okun, Arthur M. "Comment." *Rev. Econ. and Statis.*, suppl. (February 1963), pp. 72–77.

Patinkin, Don. "Price Flexibilty and Full Employment." In *Readings in Monetary Theory*, edited by F. A. Lutz and L. W. Mints. Homewood, Ill.: Irwin, 1951. Revised version of an article originally published in *A.E.R.* (September 1948), pp. 543–64.

Phillips, A. W. "The Relation between Unemployment and the Rate of Change of Money Wage Rates in the United Kingdom, 1861–1957." *Economica* (November 1958), pp. 283–99.

Pigou, A. C. "The Value of Money." *Q.J.E.* (November 1917), pp. 38–65. Reprinted in *Readings in Monetary Theory,* edited by F. A. Lutz and L. W. Mintz. Homewood, Ill.: Irwin, 1951.

———. "Economic Progress in a Stable Environment." *Economica,* n.s. (August 1947), pp. 180–88.

Sidrauski, M. "Rational Choice and Patterns of Growth in a Monetary Economy." *A.E.R.* (May 1967), pp. 534–44. (*a*)

———. "Inflation and Economic Growth." *J.P.E.* 75 (December 1967): 796–810. (*b*)

Snyder, Carl. "On the Statistical Relation of Trade, Credit and Prices." *Rev. Inst. Internat. Statis.* (October 1934), pp. 278–91.

Solow, R. M. "A Contribution to the Theory of Economic Growth." *Q.J.E.* (February 1956), pp. 65–94.

———. "On a Family of Lag Distributions." *Econometrica* (April 1960), pp. 393–406.

Stein, J. L. "Money and Capacity Growth." *J.P.E.* 74 (October 1966):451–65.

Tobin, James. "Money Wage Rates and Employment." In *The New Economics,* edited by Seymour Harris. New York: Knopf, 1947.

———. "The Interest Elasticity of Transactions Demand for Cash." *Rev. Econ. and Statis.* (August 1956), pp. 241–47.

———. "Liquidity Preference as Behavior toward Risk." *Rev. Econ. Studies* 25 (February 1958):65–86.

———. "The Monetary Interpretation of History." *A.E.R.* (June 1965). pp. 464–85. (*a*)

———. "Money and Economic Growth." *Econometrica* (October 1965), pp. 671–84. (*b*)

Tobin, James, and Brainard, William C. "Financial Intermediaries and the Effectiveness of Monetary Controls." In *Financial Markets and Economic Activity.* Cowles Foundation Monograph 21. New York: Wiley, 1967. Reprinted from *A.E.R.* (May 1963), pp. 383–400.

———. "Pitfalls in Financial Model Building." *A.E.R.* (May 1968), pp. 99–122.

Uzawa, H. "On a Neo-classical Model of Economic Growth." *Econ Studies Q.* (September 1966), pp. 1–14.

Von Neumann, John. "A Model of Economic Equilibrium." *Review of Economic Studies* 33, No. 1 (1945–46), pp. 1–9.

Walters, A. A. "A Survey of Empirical Evidence." In *Money in Britain, 1959–1969,* edited by David R. Croome and Harry G. Johnson. London: Oxford University Press, 1970, pp. 39–68.

INDEX

Allais, M., 44
Andersen, L. C., 47
Anticipated values, 55
Assets, *see* Wealth
Autonomous expenditure, 15, 20, 30, 35, 53

Bailey, M. J., 44
Baumol, W. J., 23
Brainard, W., 21
Bronfenbrenner, M., 21
Brunner, K., 11, 28

Cagan, P., 11, 31, 42, 44, 47
Capital, physical, 30, 36–37, 49
   see also Wealth
Chase, S. B. Jr., 21
Chow, G. C., 53
Consumption function:
   effect of wealth on, 16, 18, 40, 48
   elasticity of, 52
   in equations, 29–30, 34–35, 39
   factors affecting, 40
   stability of, 15
Culbertson, J. M., 1

Davidson, Paul, 32
Douglas, Major C. H., 16n

Equilibrium, long-run, 15–16, 30, 44, 48, 55–60
Expected, *see* Anticipated values and subheads "anticipated"

Feedback, 49–51, 53–55, 59
Federal Reserve Bank of St. Louis, 37
Fisher, Irving, 4, 6, 8, 18, 35, 36, 39, 43, 44, 47
Friedberg, Stephen, 37n

Friedman, M., 1, 6, 9, 11, 13, 19, 20, 25–28, 32, 40, 42, 44, 47, 55, 58, 59

Gibson, W., 47
Goldfeld, S. M., 21
Gramley, L., 21
Gupta, S., 37

Haberler, G., 16
Heller, H. R., 53
Hendershott, P. H., 31
Hester, D., 21
Hicks, J. R., 33
Holzman, F. D., 21

Income:
   expenditure analysis
      long-run equilibrium under, 15–16, 30, 44
      and quantity theory, 15–29, 43–44
   nominal
      anticipated
         determined by history of money, 40–41
         in equations, 42
         and procyclical behavior of velocity, 42, 46
      division of change in it between prices and output, 44, 48–51
      in equations, 7, 33–35, 38, 41, 49
      influences determining, 24, 27–28
      monetary theory of, 31–43, 45–48
      rate of change in
         anticipated, 36, 38, 41, 51
         lag behind change in money, 47–48

Income (*Continued*)
in model, 56–59
in equations, 41, 49, 51, 54, 58
statistical relation to money, 46
real
anticipated in equations, 49, 53–55, 59
confusion with nominal income, 27
division with prices of, and change in nominal income, 17–19, 44, 48–51
in equations, 7, 9, 13, 23, 29, 31–34, 39, 49, 54–55, 59
as index of wealth, 11–12
in model, 55–61
and nominal money, 27
as percentage of full-employment level, 49
rate of change in
anticipated, in equations, 36–38, 40, 49
anticipated, in monetary theory of nominal income, 36–37, 42
in equations, 49
in model, 55–61
and in real money stock, 46
seems to move with real rate of interest, 38
steady for any given country, 37
and real money stock, 46
why excluded from investment function, 30
Induced expenditure, 20, 30, 35
Inflation and deflation, 12, 21*n*, 40, 50
Interest rate:
nominal, anticipated, 23–25, 35
and anticipated rate of change in prices, 36, 42, 45, 58
in equations, 13, 23, 29–39, 41–42, 52–53

Interest rate (*Continued*)
historical connection with price behavior, 37
how determined in income-expenditure analysis, 20–22
lag at turning points of change in money, 47
as link between money change and real income, 26, 28
and monetary theory of nominal income, 36–40, 42
pegging of, 26
and supply of money, 31, 38, 53–54
real, 36–37, 39–40, 42, 58
anticipated, real and monetary theory of nominal income, 36–40, 42
Intermediate transactions, 7
Investment as fraction of national income, 36–37
Investment function:
elasticity of, 52
in equations, 29, 33–35, 39
in income-expenditure analysis, 15
Investment opportunities, deficiency of, 25

Johnson, H. G., 16, 44, 58
Jordan, J. I., 47

Kaufman, G., 47
Keynes, J. M., 1, 11, 12, 15–28, 30, 32–36, 39, 43–45, 49, 50, 52, 53
Knight, Frank H., 37
König, H., 53
Koyck, L. M., 44

Laurent, R., 6*n*
Leijonhufvud, A., 16, 17, 22, 35
Levhari, D., 44
Liquidity preference:
absolute, 15, 21–29, 33, 52
definition, 12

Liquidity preference (*Continued*)
  factors determining value attached
    to, 12–13
  see also Money, real, demand
    for
Liquidity trap, Keynesian short-run
  vs. long-run, 24–27

Malthus, T. R., 16
Marshall, Alfred,10, 16–19
Martin, P. W., 16
Marty, A., 58
Measured, *see* subheads "actual"
Meiselman, D., 28, 40
Meltzer, A. H., 1, 11, 46
Mitchell, W. C., 6
Monetary theory of nominal income,
  31–43, 45–48
Money:
  definition of, 6, 9, 22
  functions of, 8–10
  high-powered, 10–11, 21*n*, 38*n*
  nominal
    defined, 1–2
    effect of increase on nominal
     income, 28, 46–47, 51
    in equations, 4, 7, 9, 30–34, 38,
     41–42, 51, 59
    in quantity theory of money,
     2–3
    per unit of output, rate of
     change in, 46
    rate of change
     in equations, 42, 51, 58–59
     lead over velocity and in-
      terest rates, 47
     in model, 55–61
     and short-term fluctuations,
      47
    short-run effect of change in,
     17–20, 26–27
    supply of, 10, 17–18, 31, 38,
     53–54

Money (*Continued*)
  real
    definition, units, and relation to
     quantity theory, 2–3
    demand for, 10–15, 21–30, 48,
     53, 56–59
     by business enterprises, 14–
      15
     by ultimate wealth holders,
      11–14
     in equations, 13, 23, 29–30
     income elasticity of demand
      for, 34, 42, 46, 55
     statistical relation to real in-
      come, 46
Mundell, R. A., 44
Muth, J. F., 44

Nerlove, M., 44

Okun, A. M., 26
Output, *see* Income, real

Patinkin, D., 16, 44
Permanent, *see* Anticipated values
  and subheads "anticipated"
Phillips, A. W., 32
Phillips curve, 32
Pigou, A. C., 16, 17, 25
Policy in Great Depression, 19
Price level, outcome of monetary
  and real forces, 27
Price rigidity or flexibility:
  in income-expenditure theory, 15–
   16, 20–21, 23, 26, 28–29, 32,
   44, 50
  in quantity theory, 18
Prices:
  anticipated rate of change in
   assumed zero in two theories,
    39
   and consumption, 40
   in equations, 13, 36, 49, 54,
    59–60

Prices (*Continued*)
and interest rates, 36, 42, 45, 58
in model, 55–61
and monetary theory of nominal income, 36, 42
and procyclical behavior of velocity, 42, 46
division with output of a change in income, 17–19, 44, 48–51
in equations, 4–5, 7, 9, 32–33, 49, 54, 59
and nominal money per unit of output, 46
and quantity theory, 2–3
speed of adjustment to change in nominal income, 18–19
unemployment and rate of change in, 32

Quantity equations, 4–6, 8–11, 15, 17
Quantity theory of money:
assumes given real income, 31
compared with income-expenditure analysis, 43–44
and primacy of nonmonetary forces for real income in long run, 27
status and statement of, 1–3
and transmission mechanism to total spending, 27–29
Rates of return, anticipated, 12–14
see also Interest rates
Ratio money stock to income
in equations, 9, 23
factors influencing, 27
in income-expenditure analysis, 17–20

Savings function, *see* Consumption function

Schwartz, A. J., 1, 6, 9, 11, 27, 28, 47
Sidrauski, M., 44
Snyder, C., 6
Social credit, 16n
Solow, R. W., 44
Stein, J. L., 58

Tobin, J., 16, 21, 23–26, 44

Unemployment, 32, 50
Uzawa, H., 44

Velocity of circulation of goods, 5n
Velocity of circulation of money:
cyclical timing, 42, 46–47
definition, 2
in equations, 4–7, 33, 38, 41–42
in Keynes, 26
in model, 57
in quantity theory, 5–6, 15
Vertical integration, 8
Von Neumann, J., 37

Wage rigidity in income-expenditure theory, 18–19, 23, 32n
Walras, L., 31, 32, 44, 45, 48, 55
Walrasian equations, *see* author entry
Walters, A. A., 46
Wealth:
and consumption, 18, 20, 24–25, 40, 48
and demand for money, 11–14, 30, 48
human vs. nonhuman, 12, 36–37
income as index of, 11–12
narrower range of assets stressed in Keynesian than quantity theory, 28
and quantity equations, 5n, 7–8
ratio of currency to, 21n
see also Capital, physical